IMAGES OF ITALY

COMPANION TO

LA VIAGGIATRICE (THE TRAVELER)

BACKPACKING ITALY

Photos by Anna Castiglioni

Cinque Terre, Riomaggiore

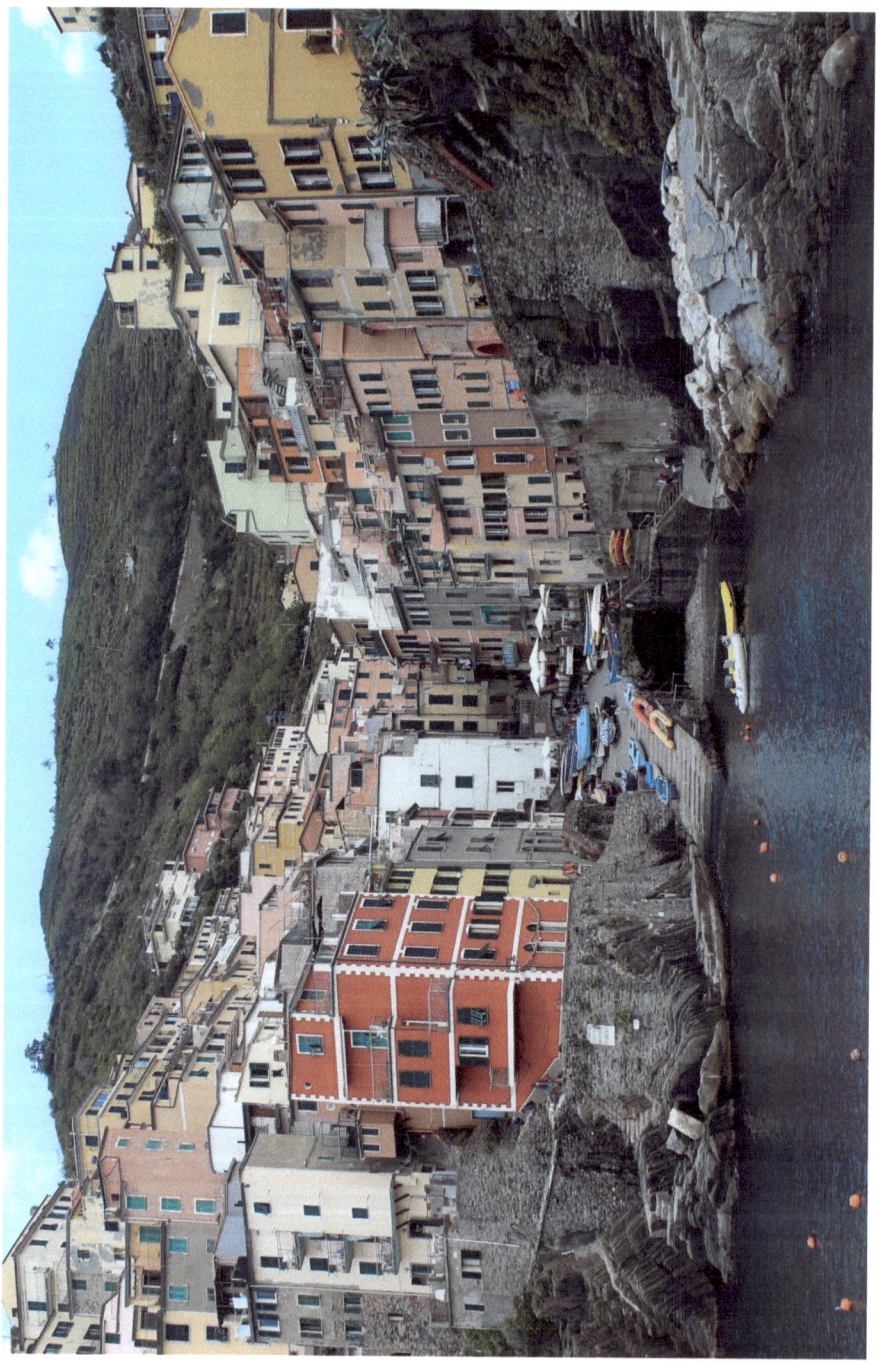

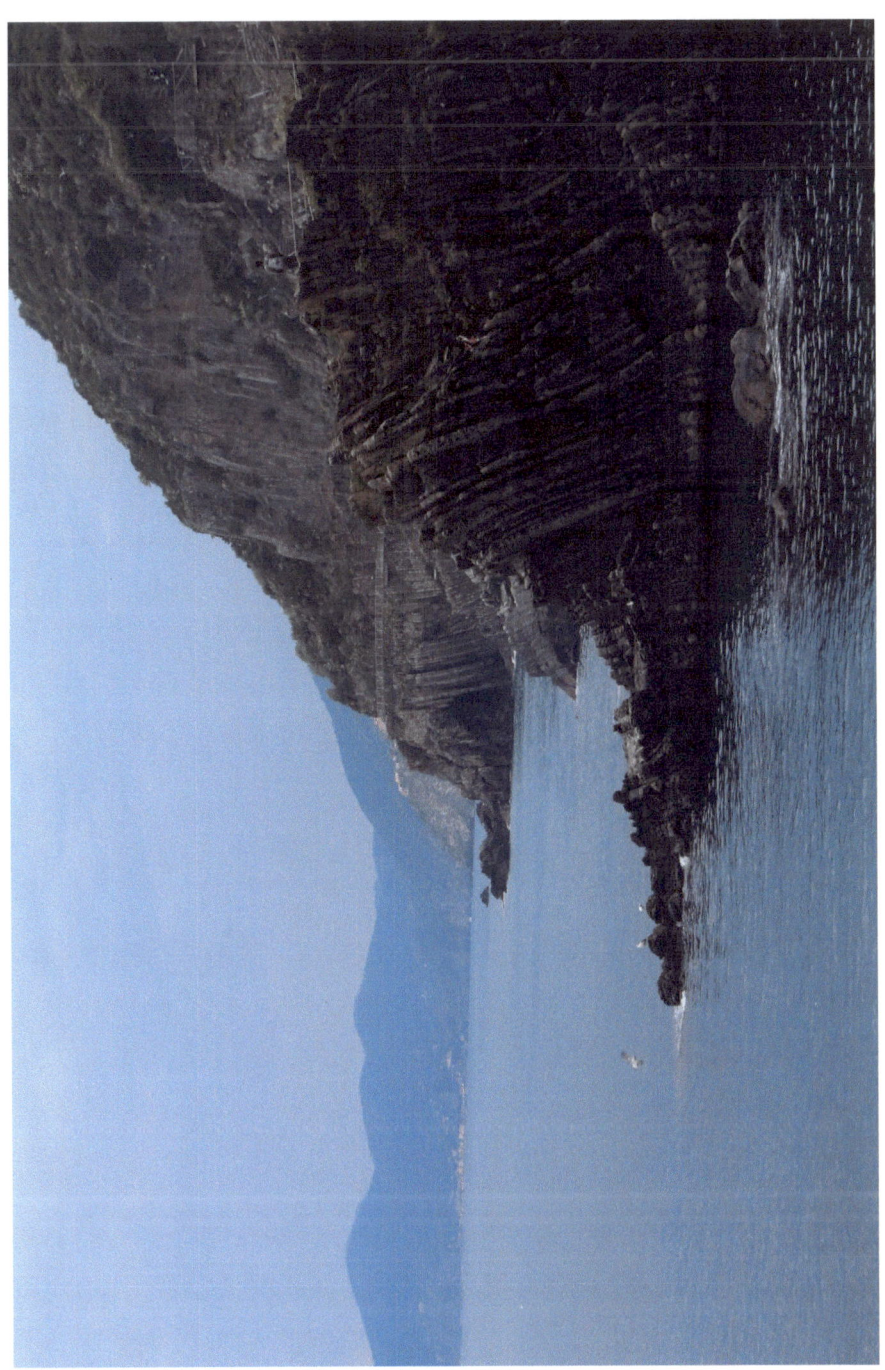

© Anna Castiglioni, 3

Cinque Terre, Monterosso Al Mare

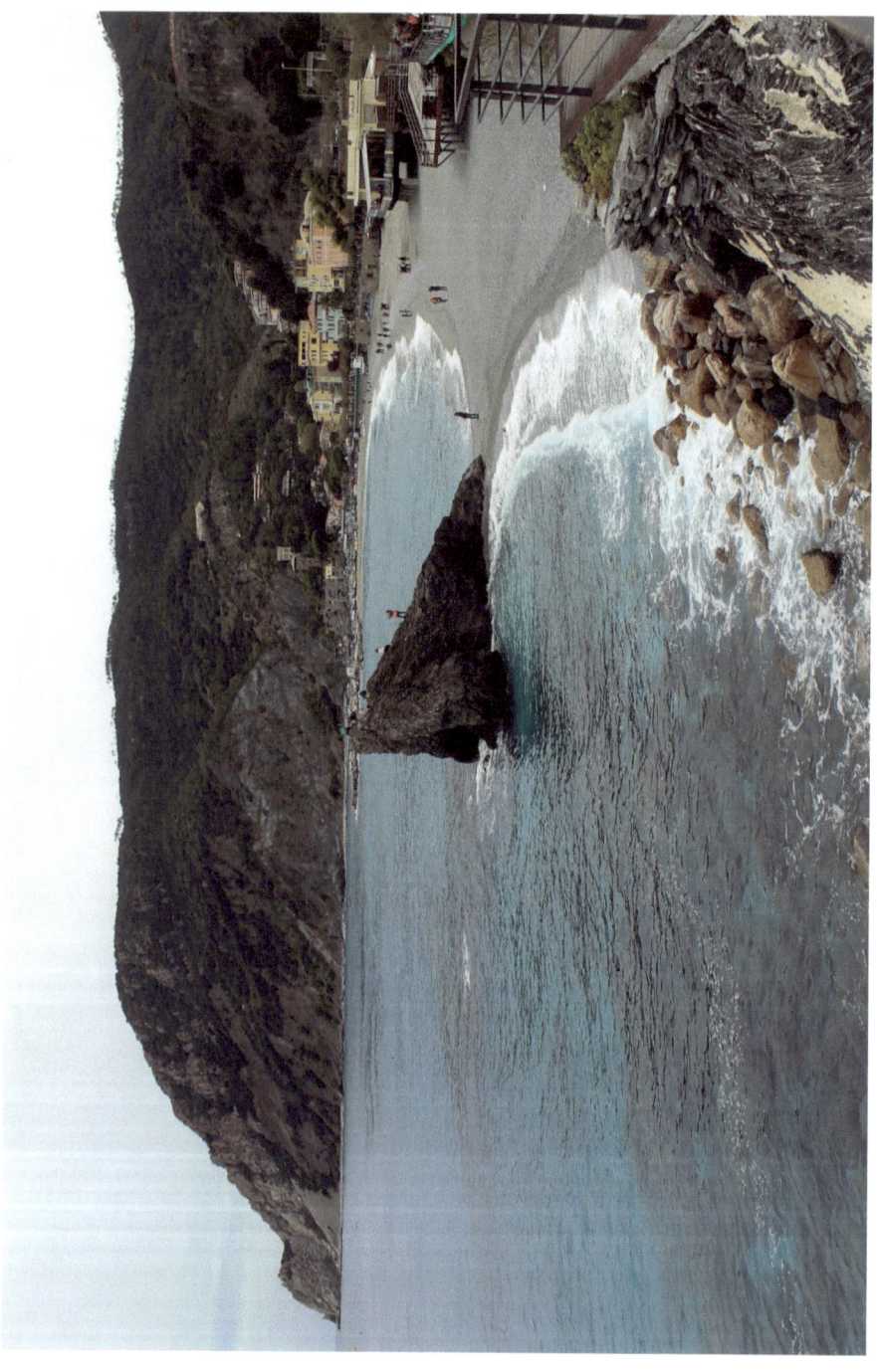

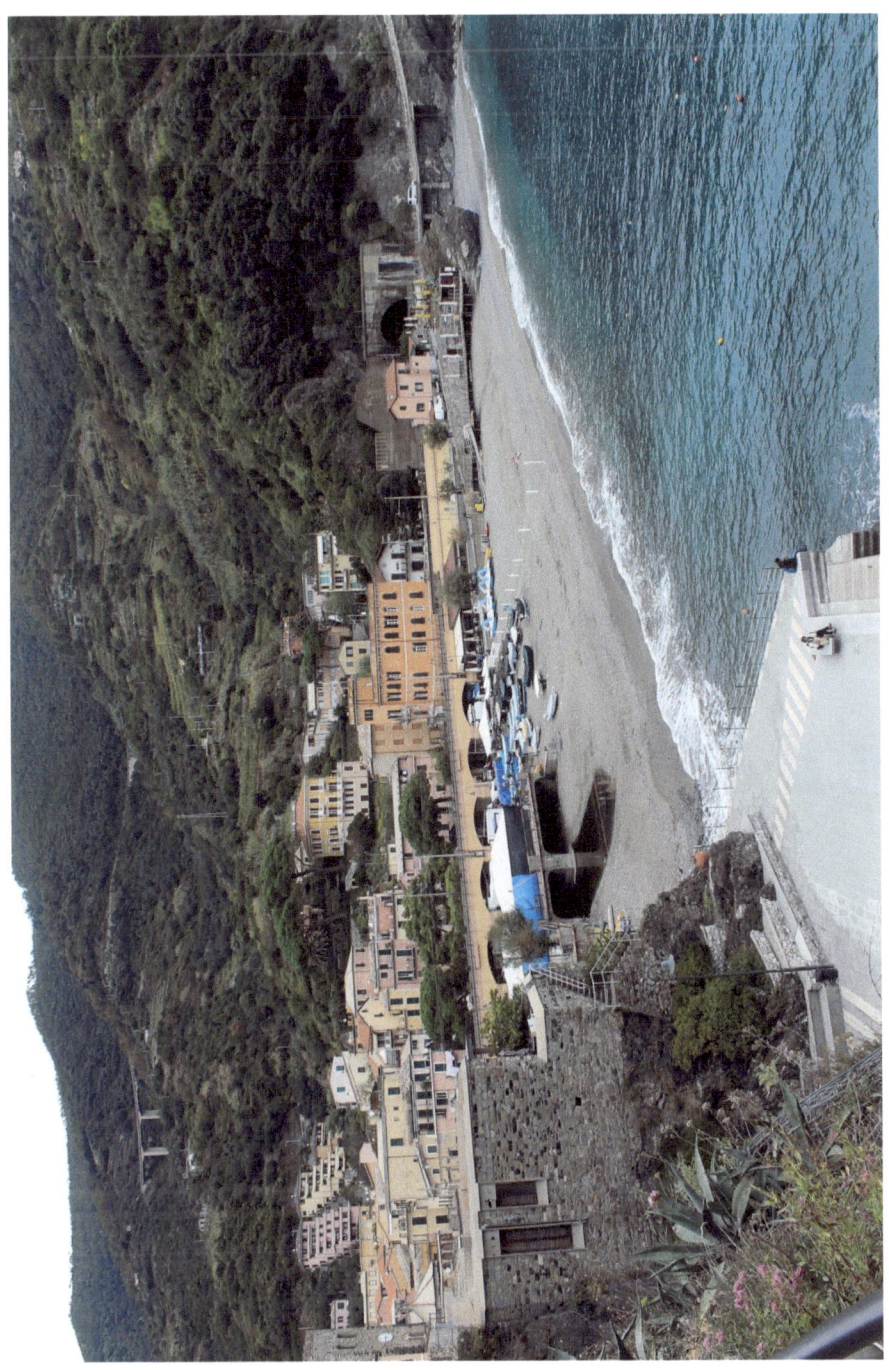

© Anna Castiglioni, 5

Genoa

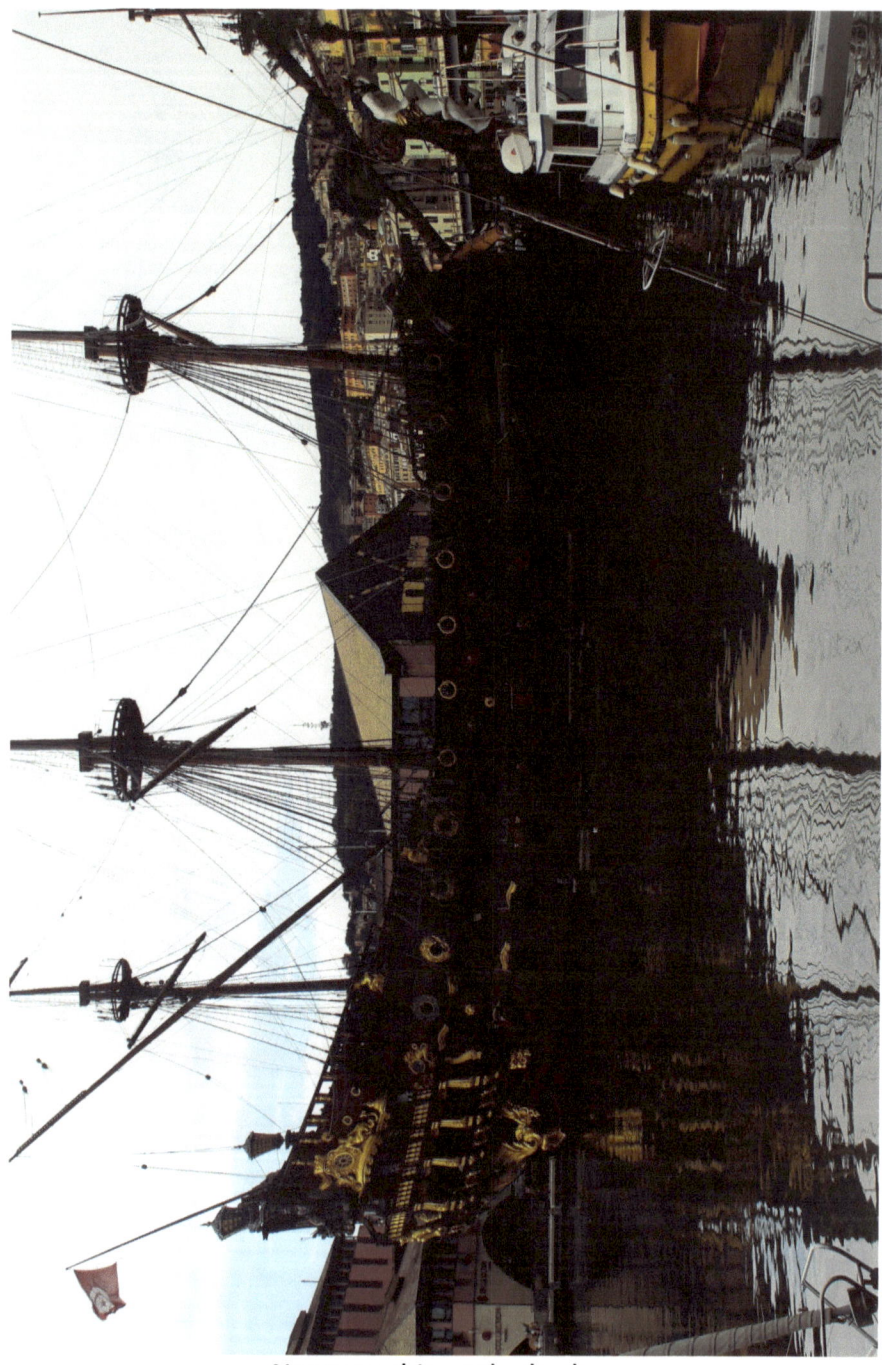

Neptune ship at the harbor

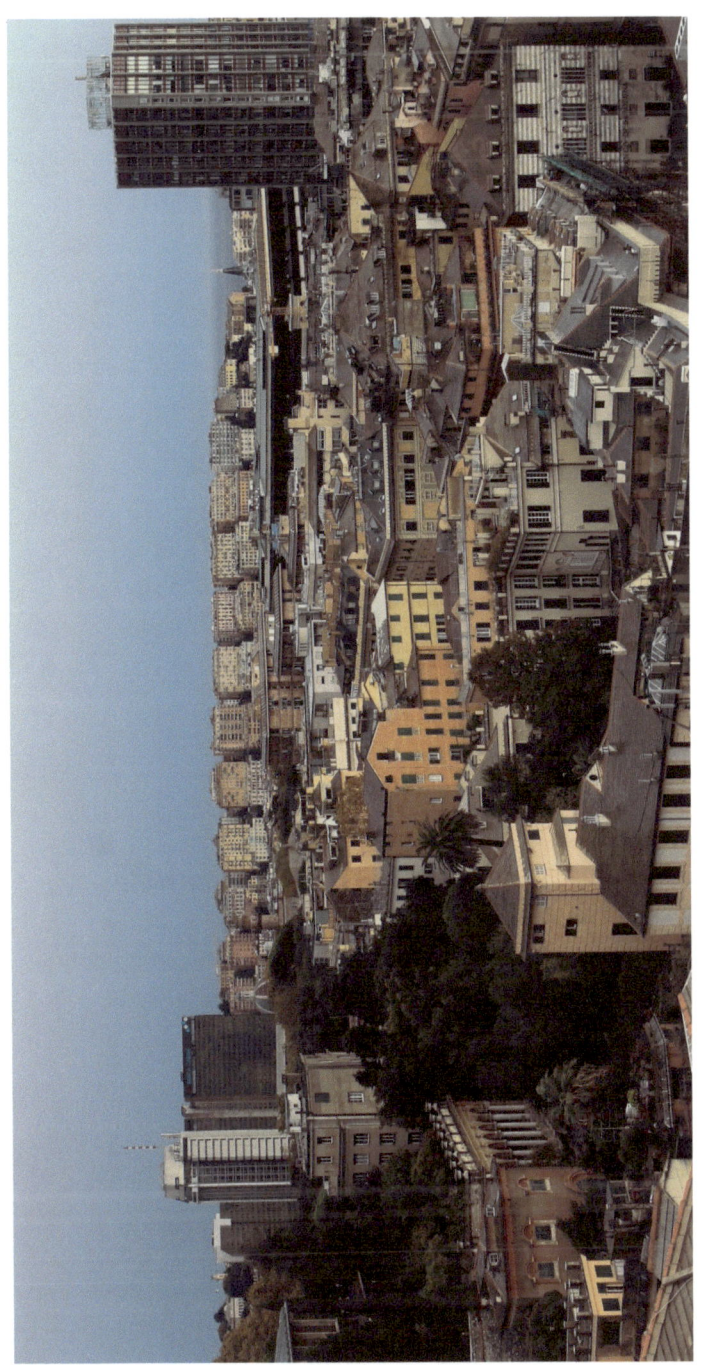

Spianata del Castelletto

Milano

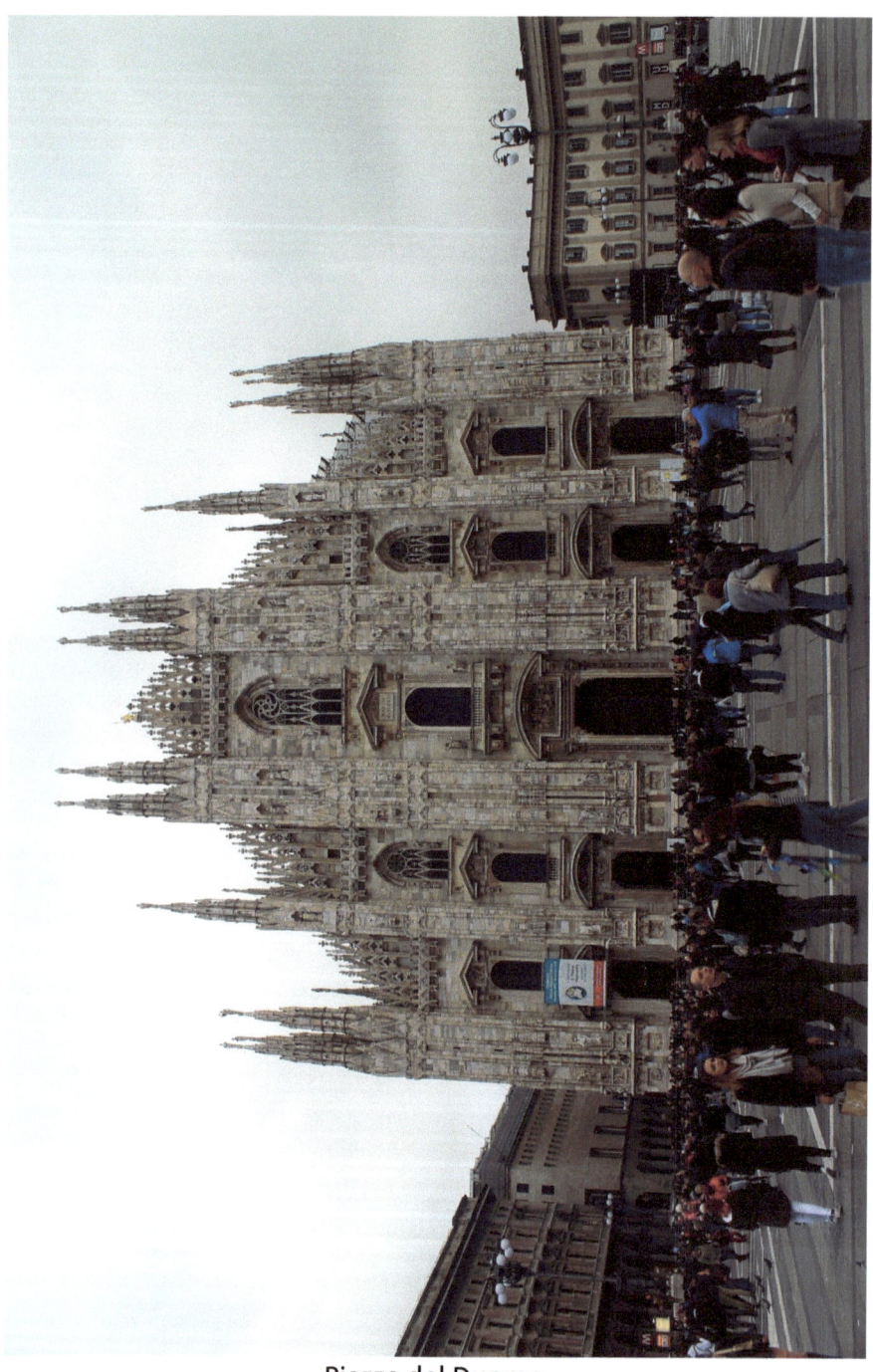

Piazza del Duomo

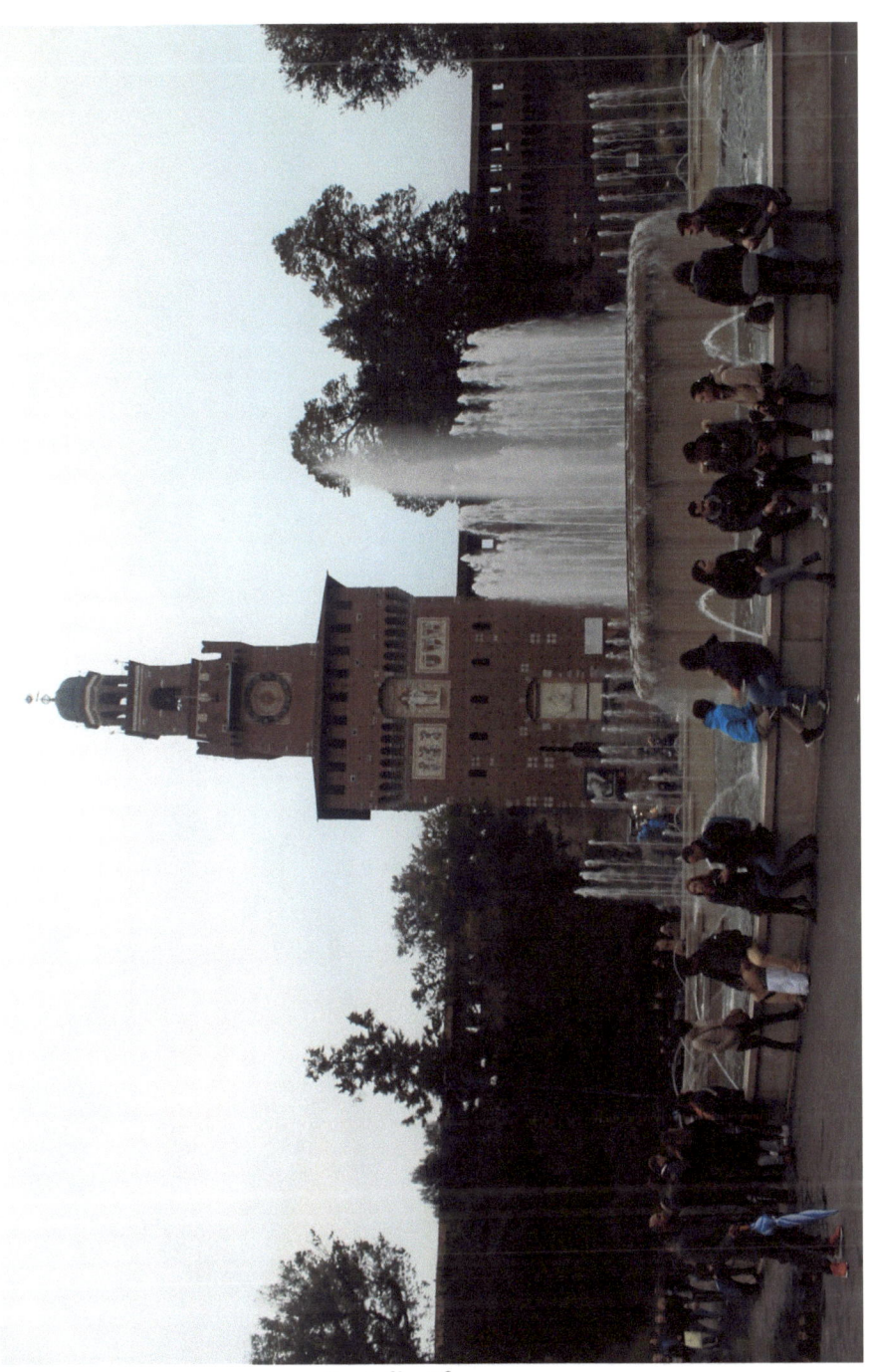

Castello Sforzesco

Verona

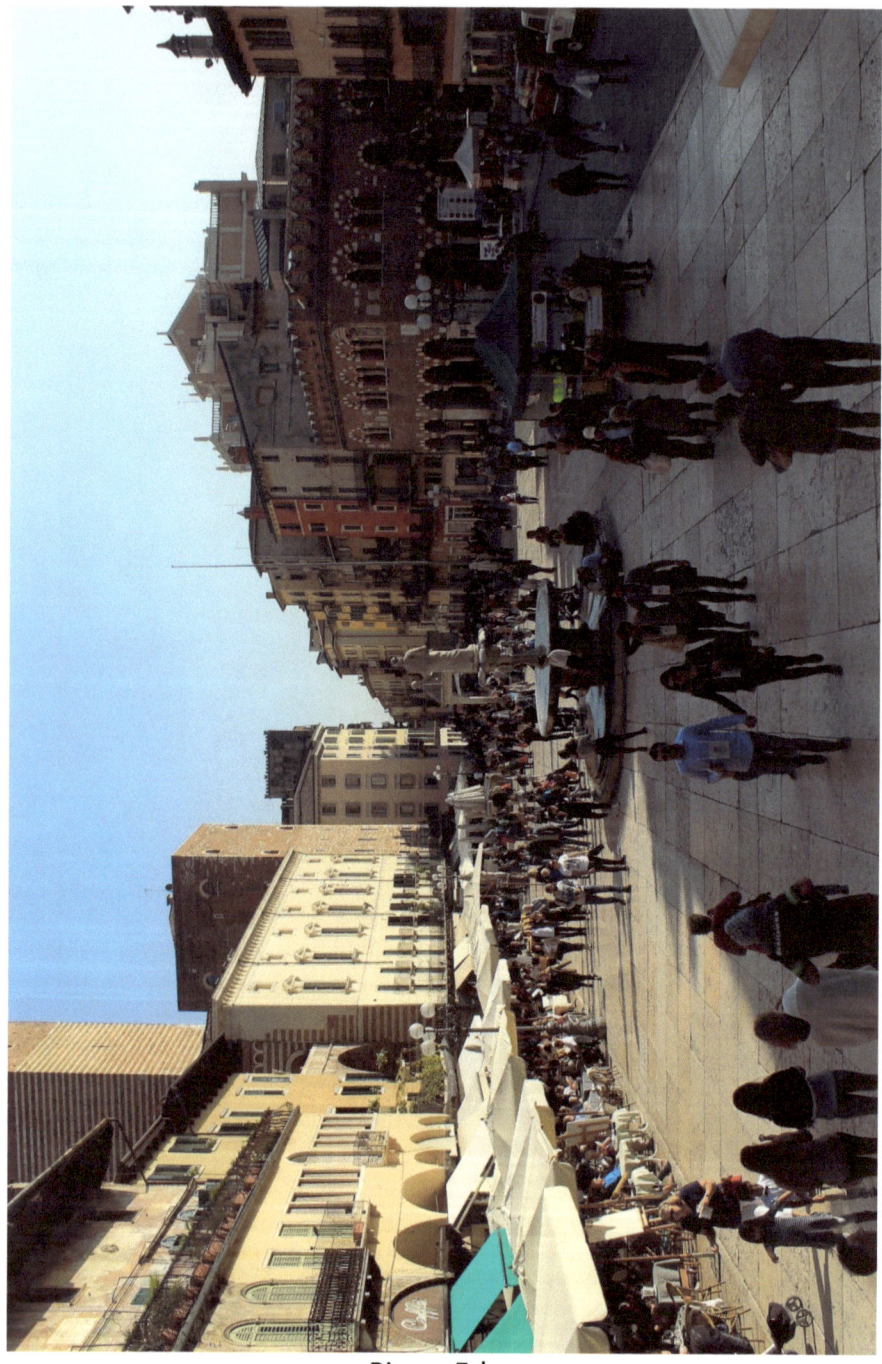

Piazza Erbe

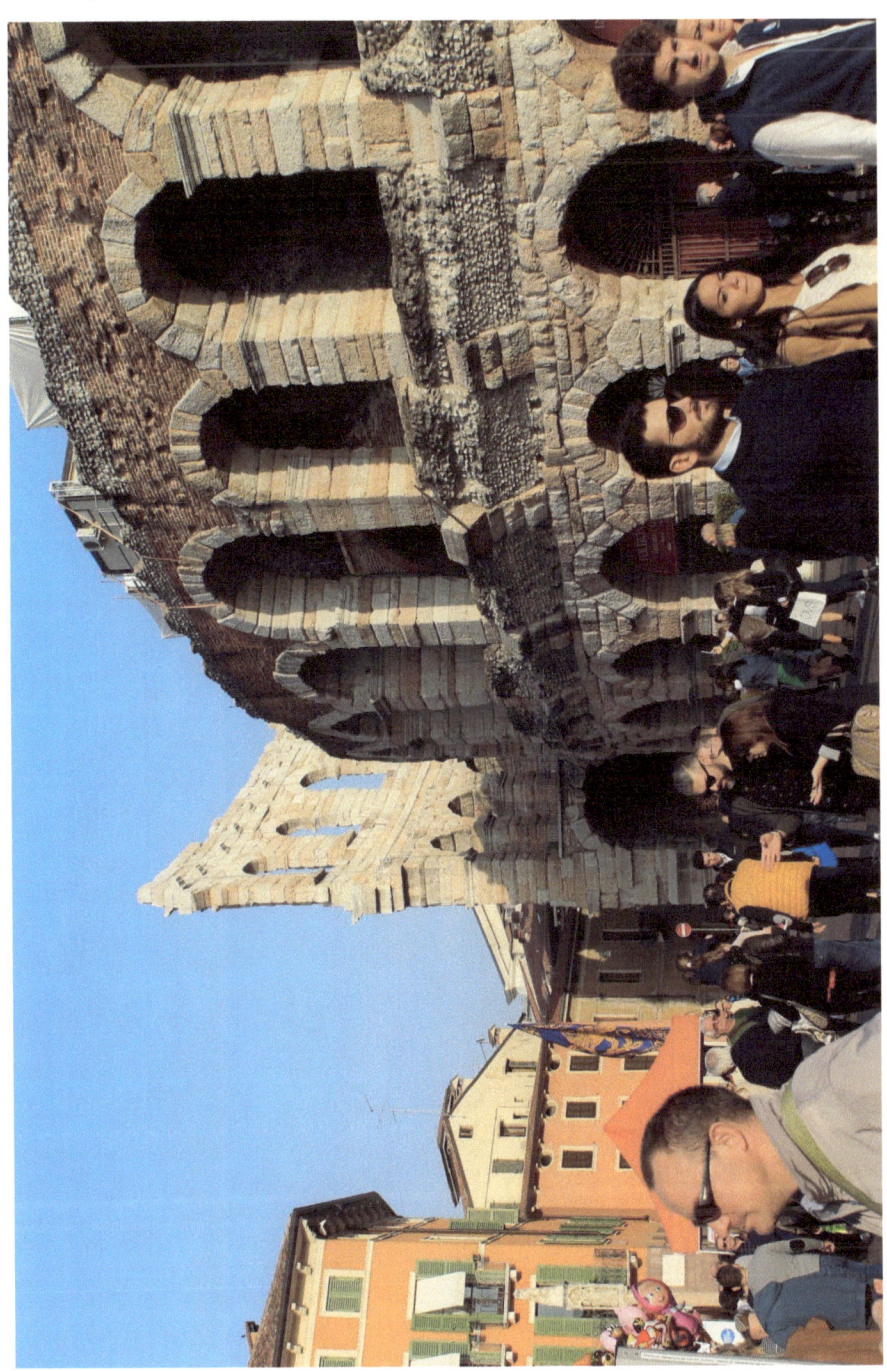

Piazza Bra, Arena

© Anna Castiglioni, 11

Lucca

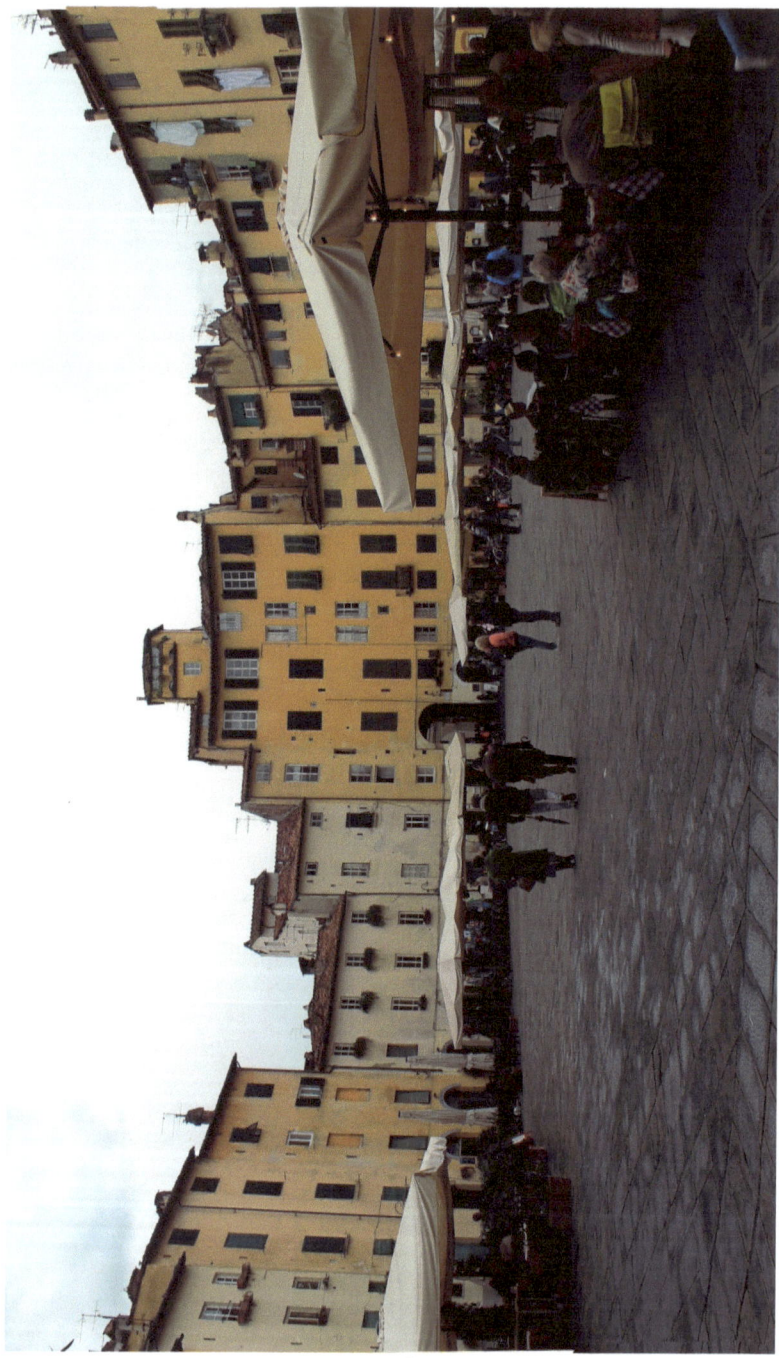

Piazza Anfiteatro

Siena

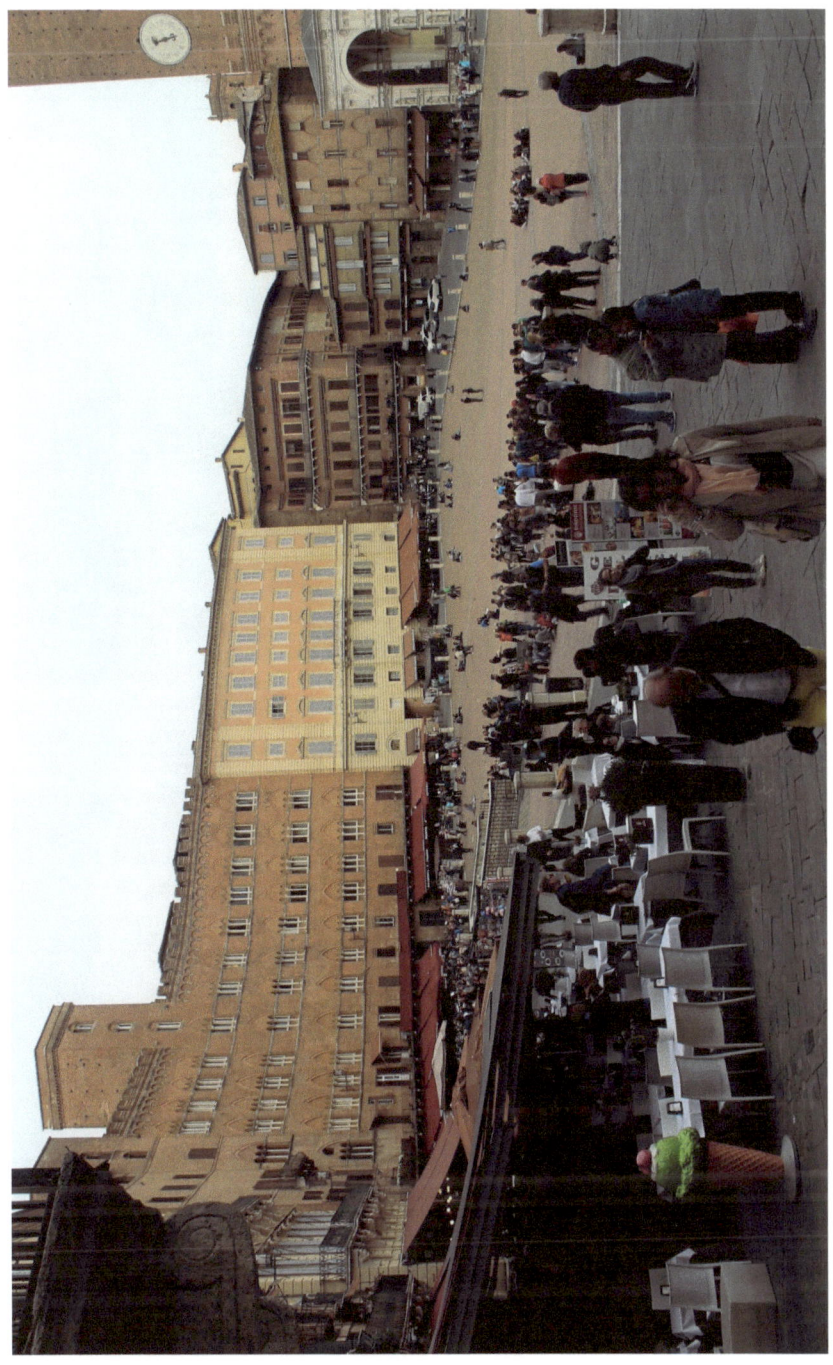

Piazza del Campo

Venezia (Venice)

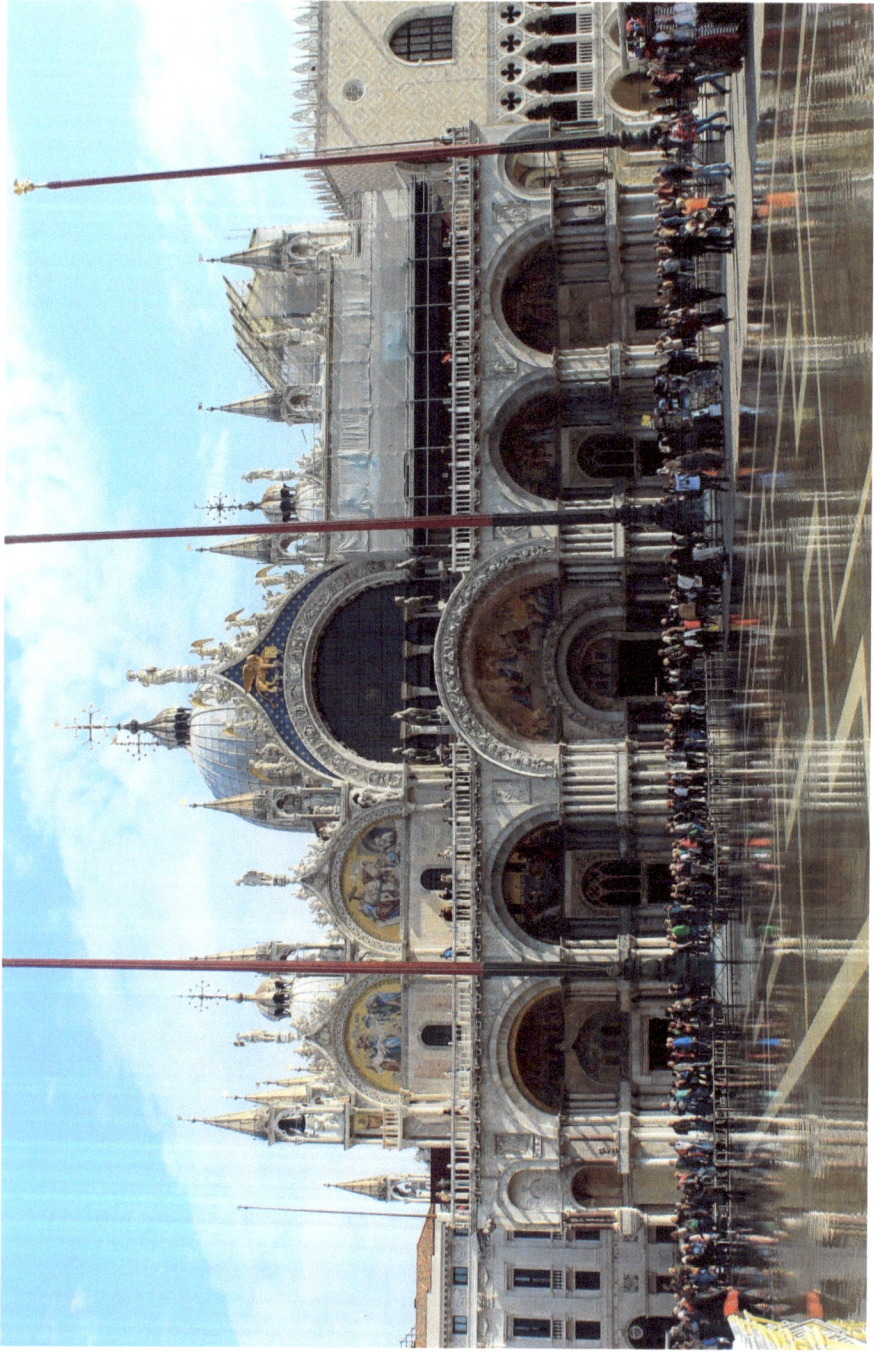

Piazza San Marco flooding

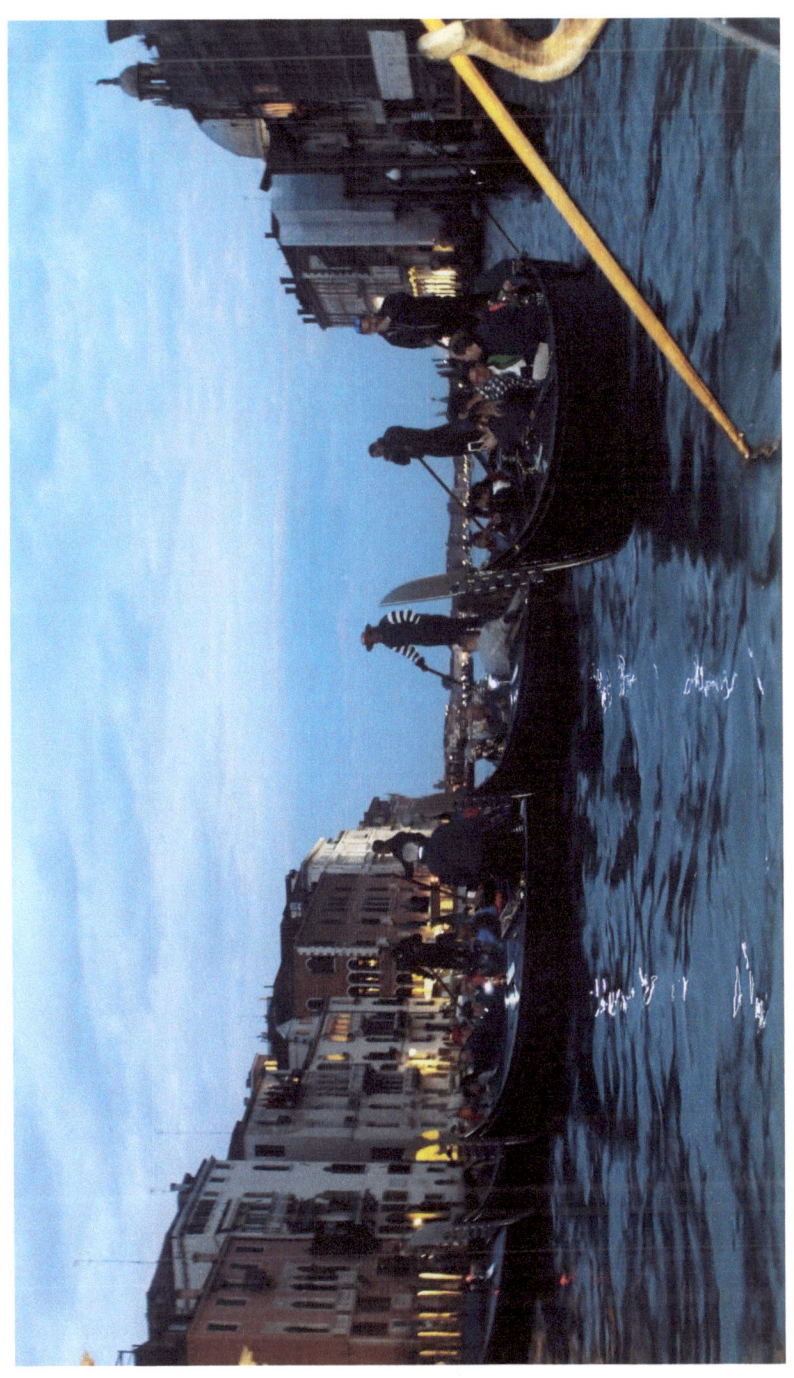

Gondola ride with serenade

Venezia (Venice)

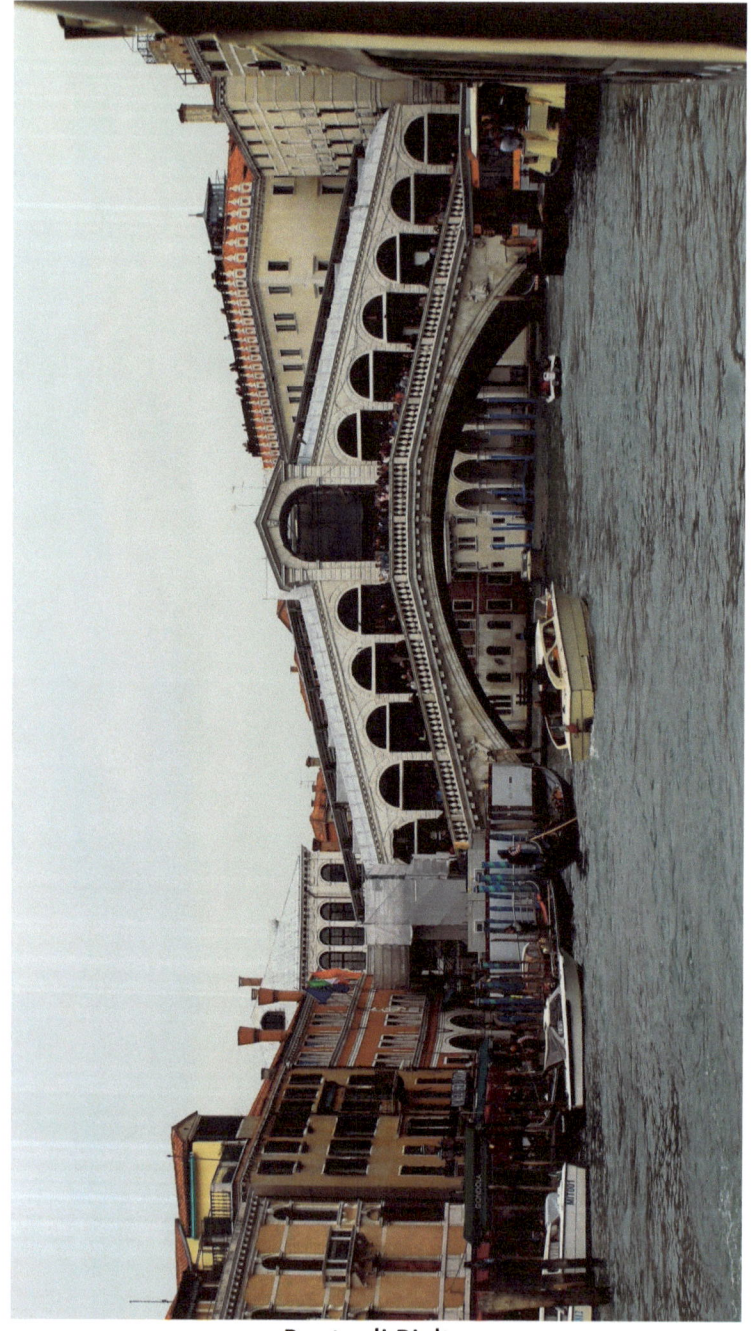

Ponte di Rialto

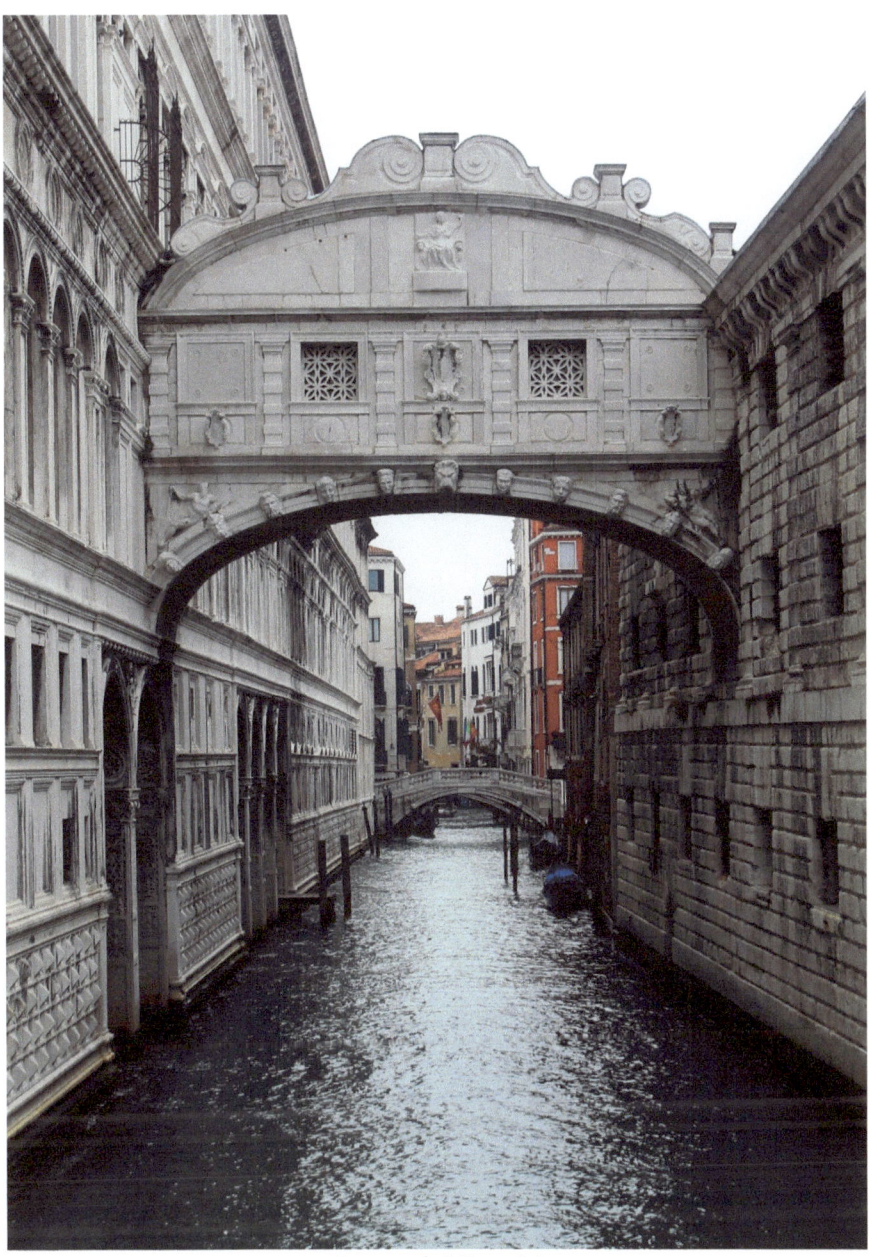

Ponte dei Sospiri

Firenze (Florence)

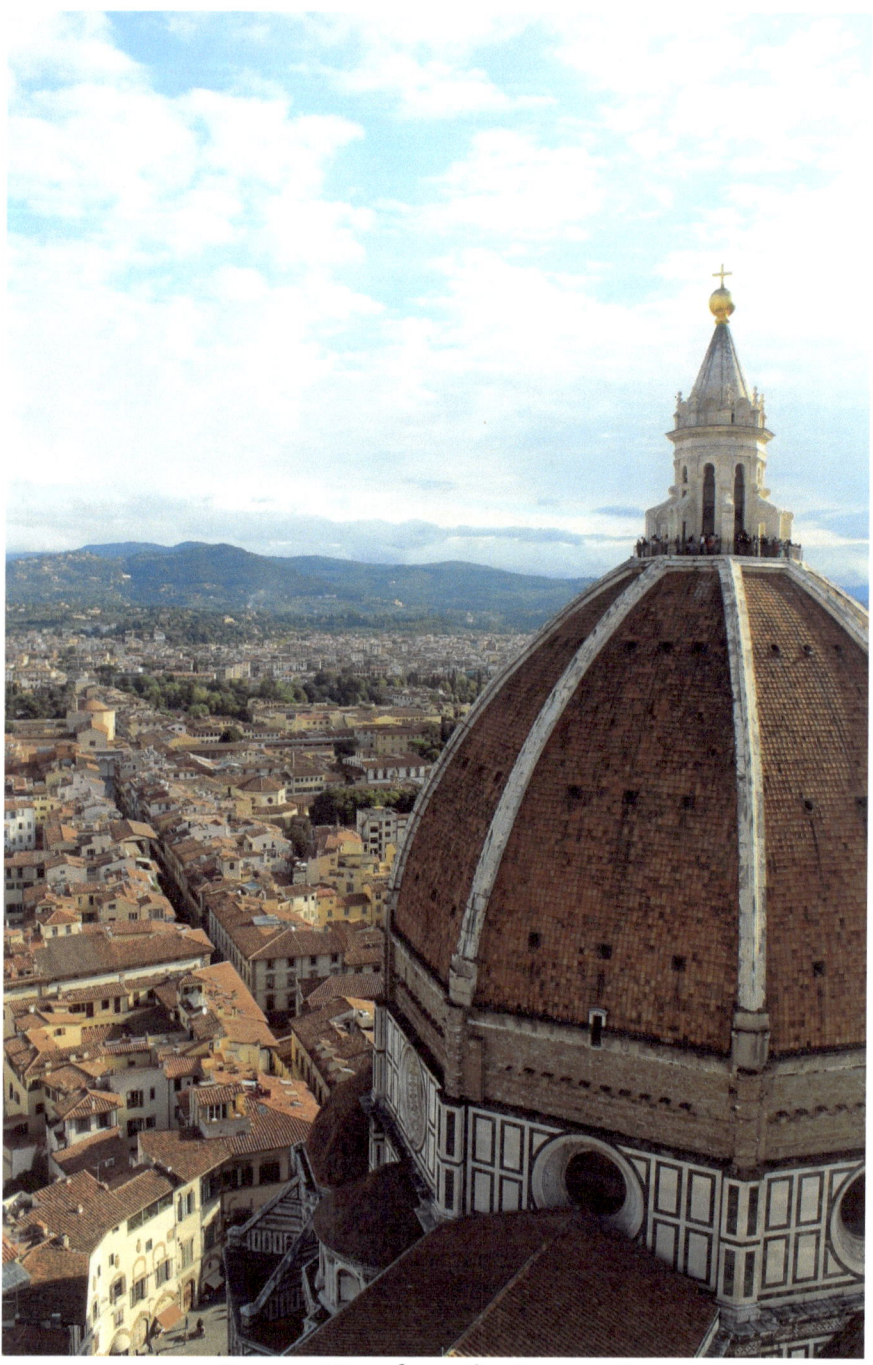

Duomo, View from the Campanile

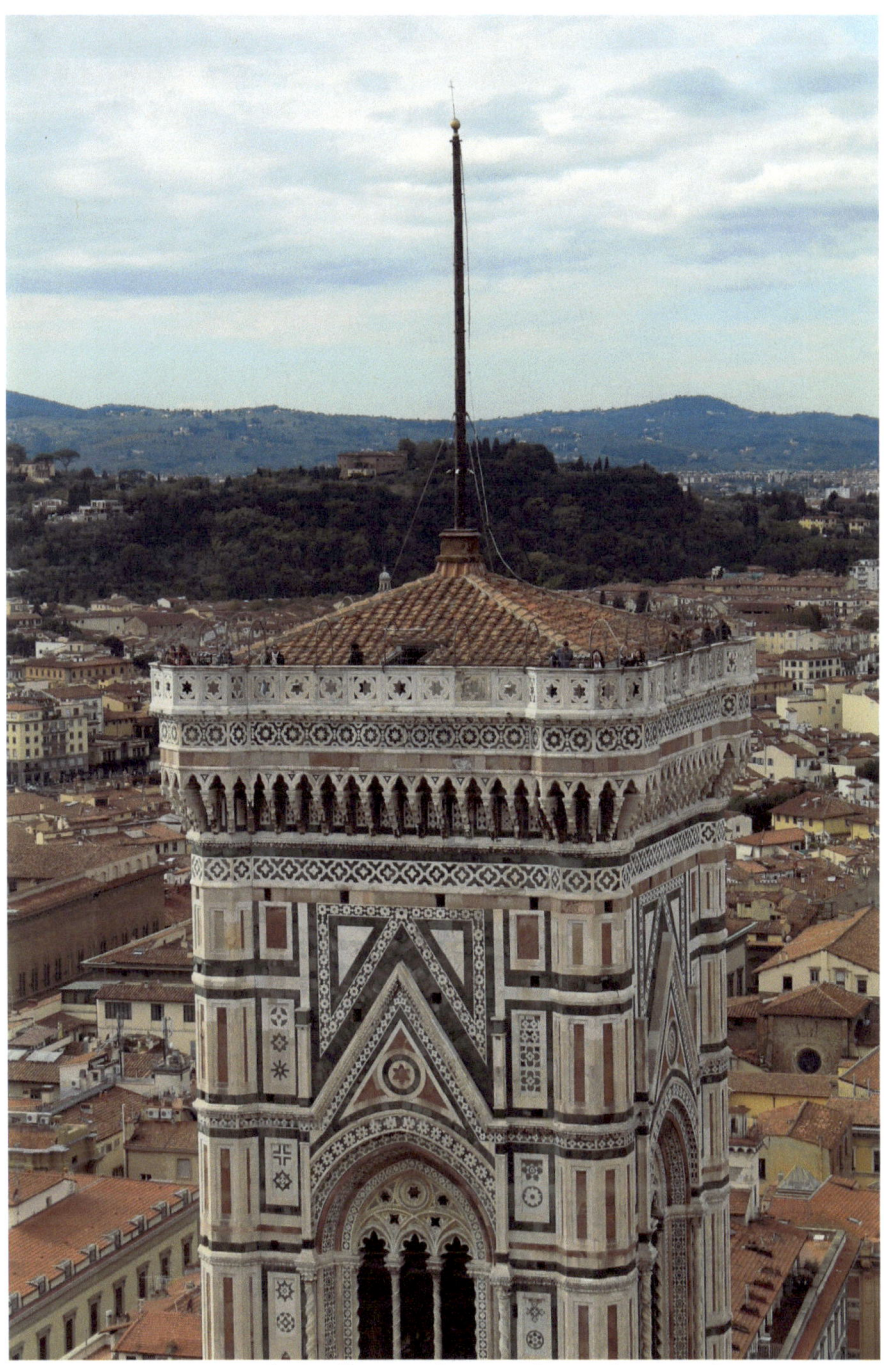

Campanile (Bell Tower), View from the copula

Firenze (Florence)

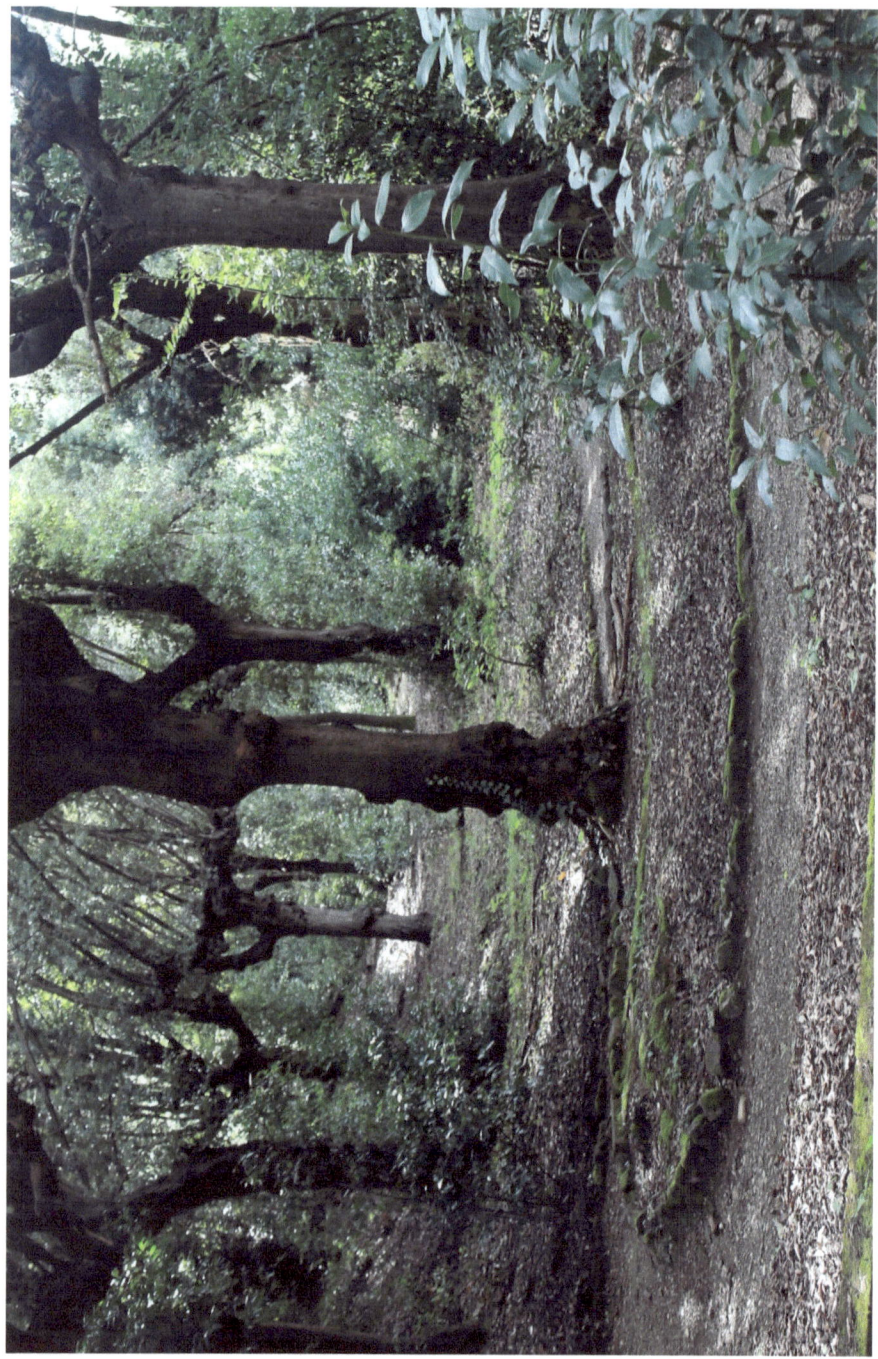

Forest in the Boboli Gardens

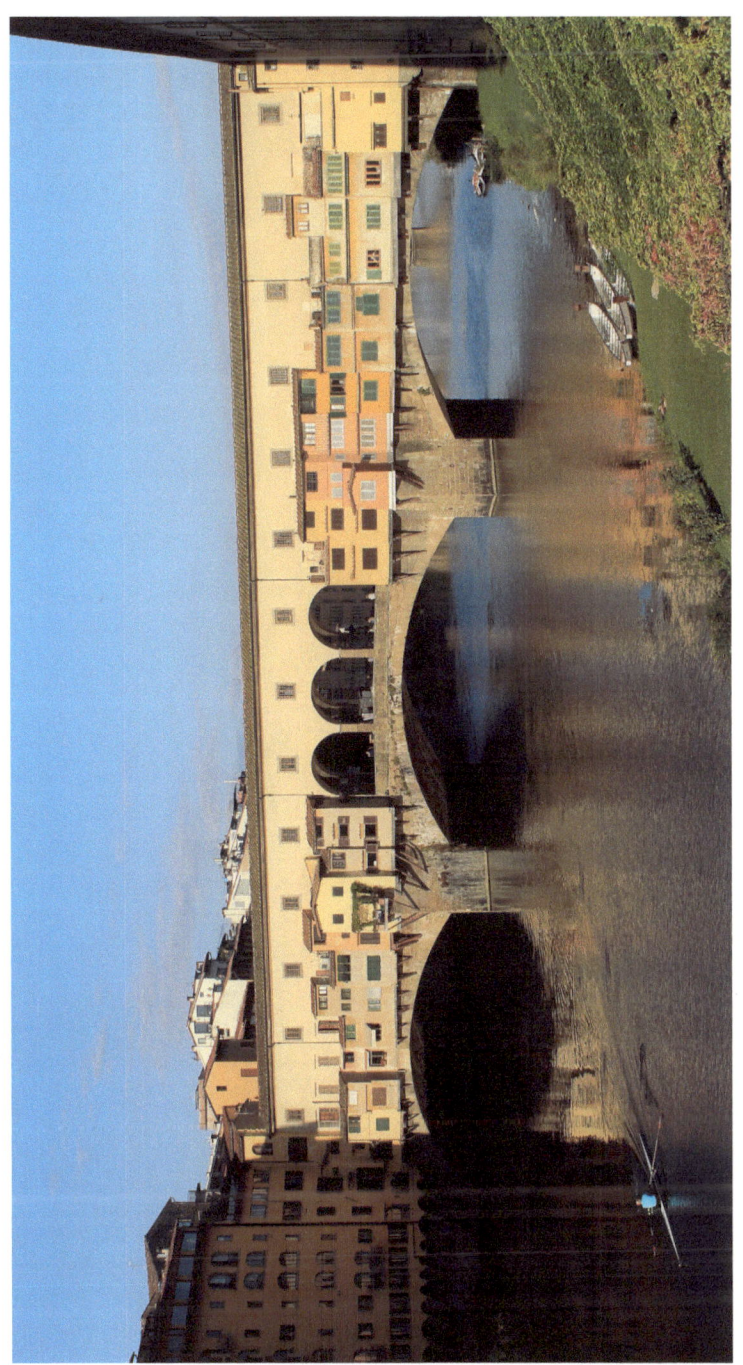

Ponte Vecchio

Roma (Rome)

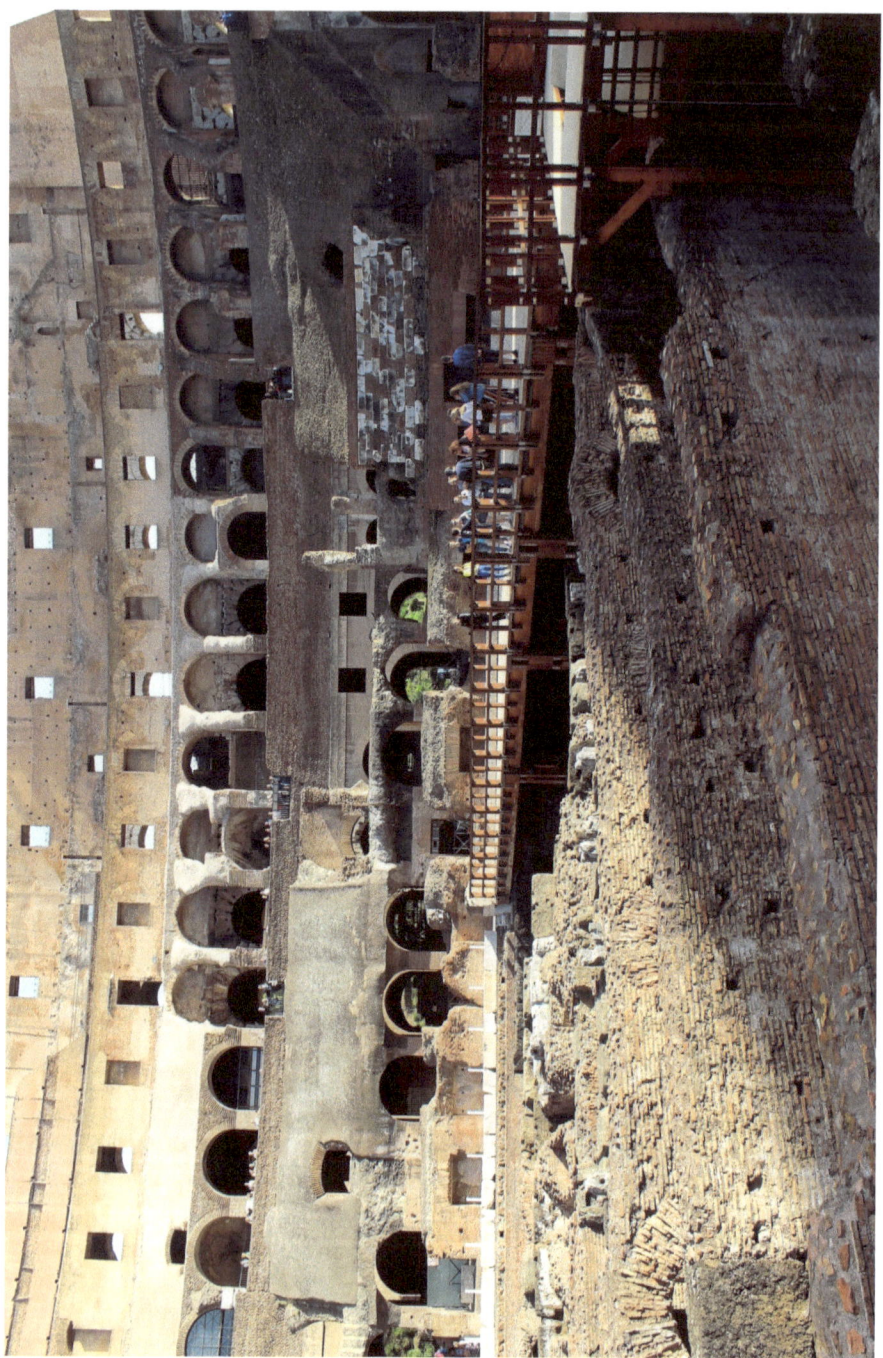

Colosseum interior and underground

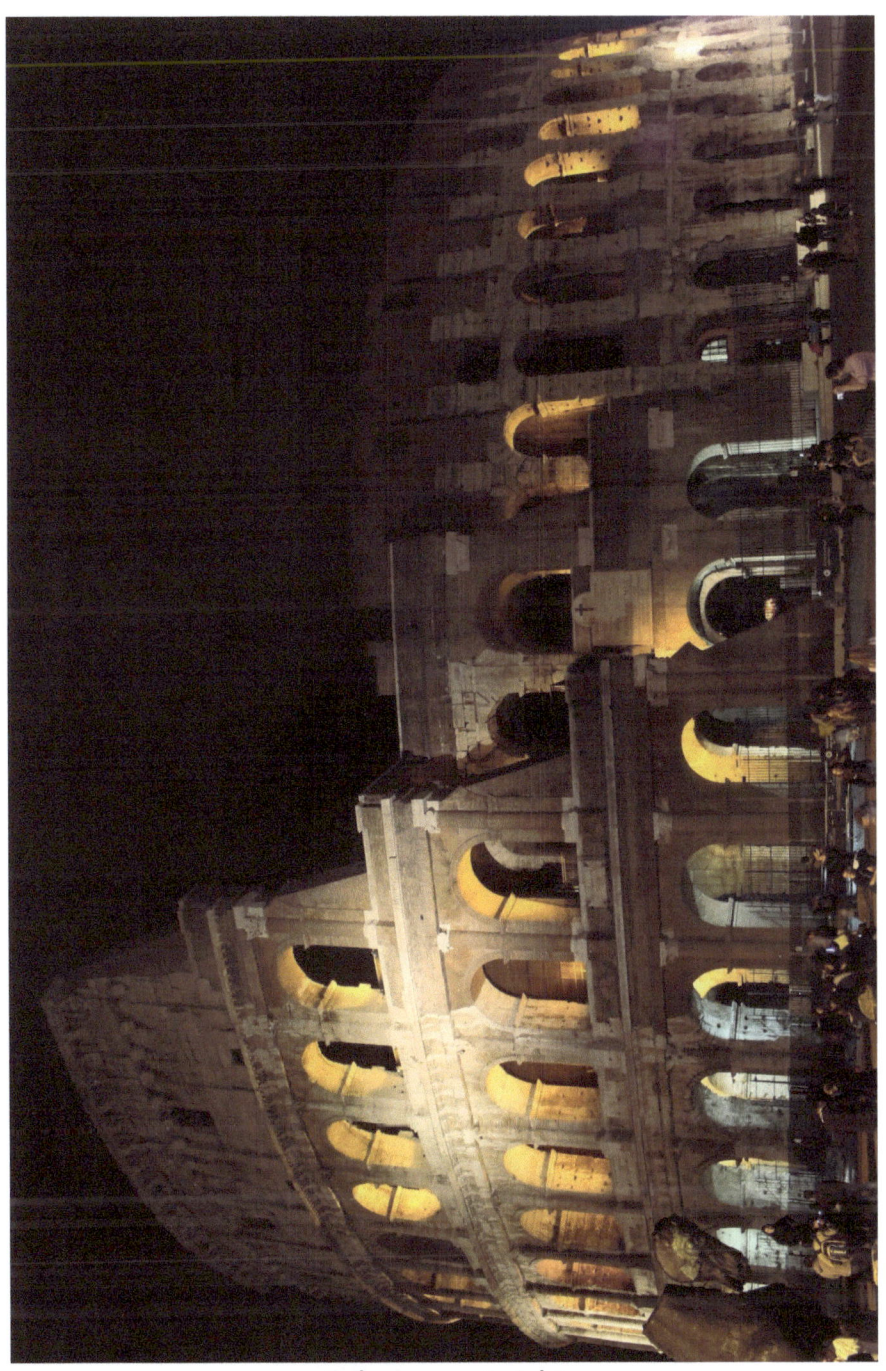

Colosseum at night

Roma (Rome)

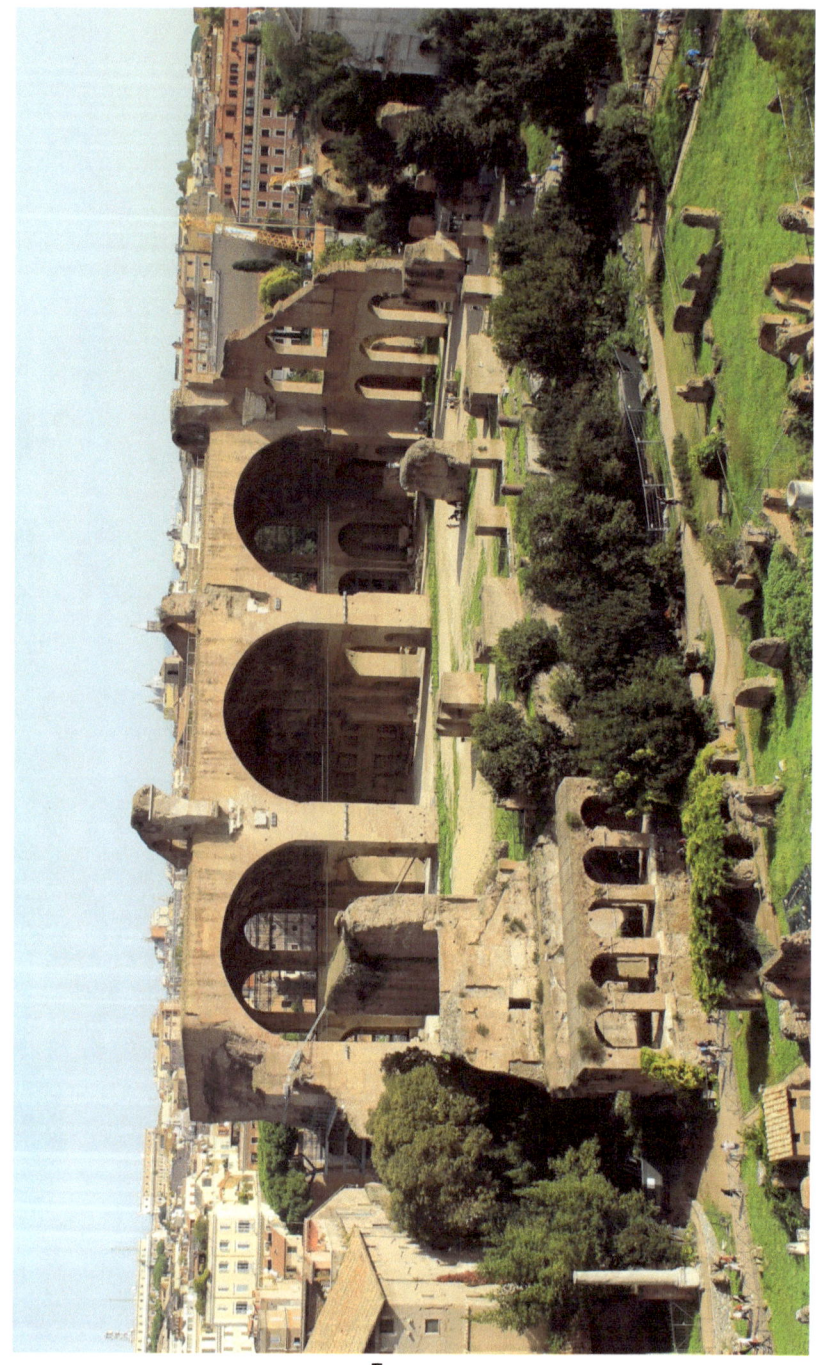

Forum

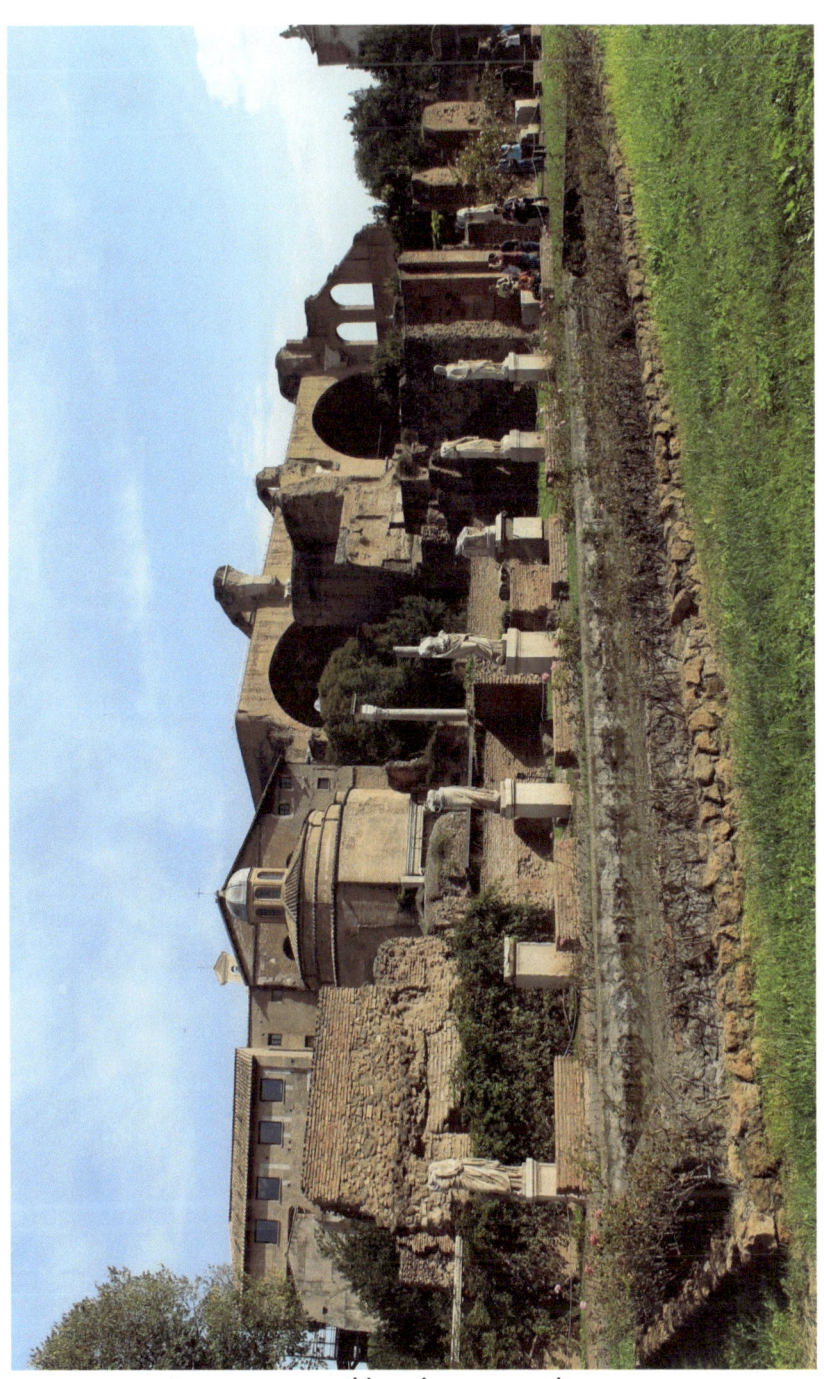

Forum, statues' heads were stolen away

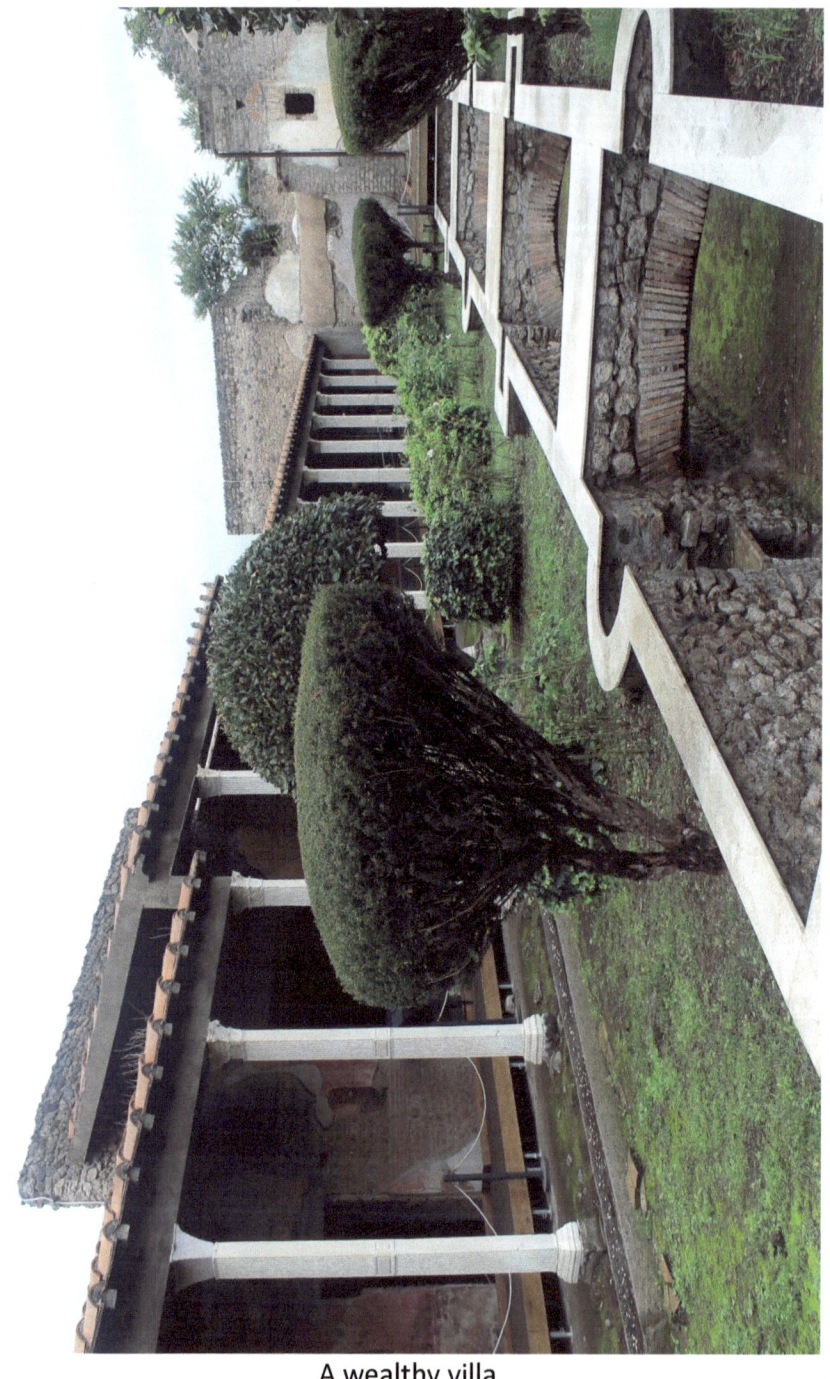

A wealthy villa

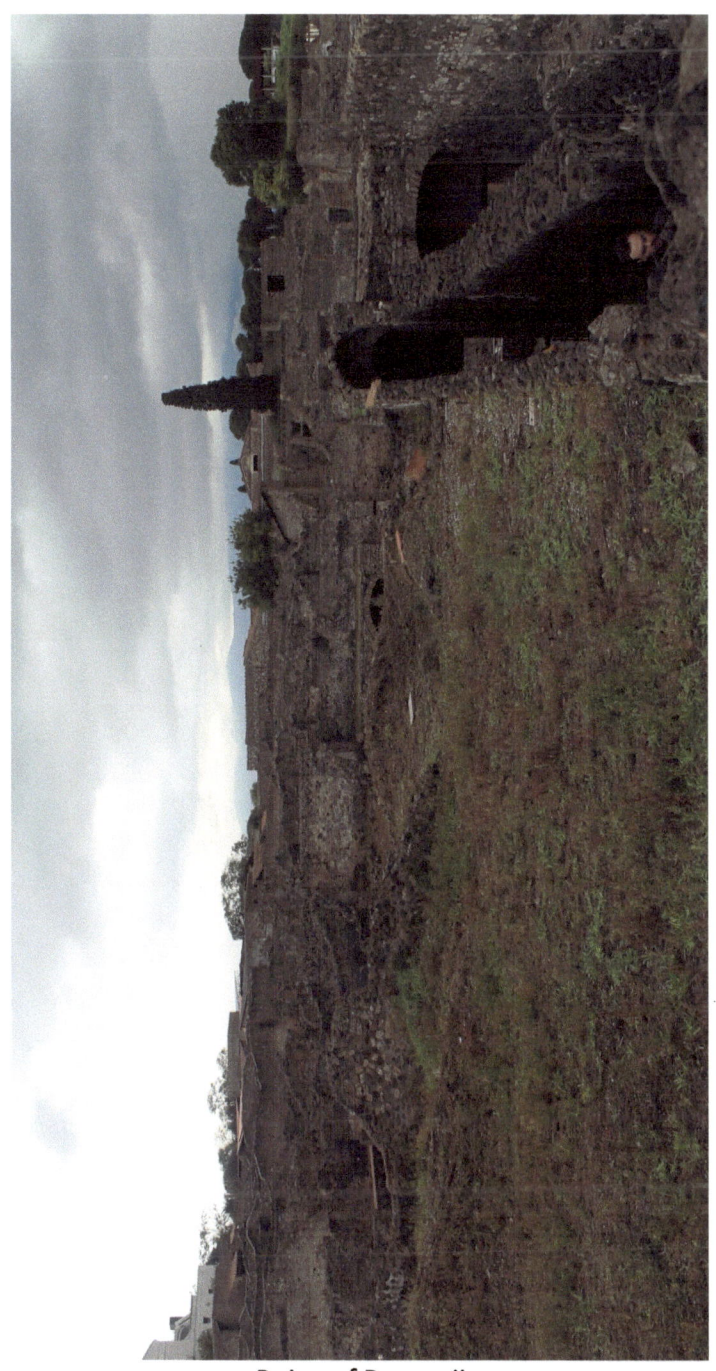

Ruins of Pompeii

© Anna Castiglioni, 27

Amalfi Coast

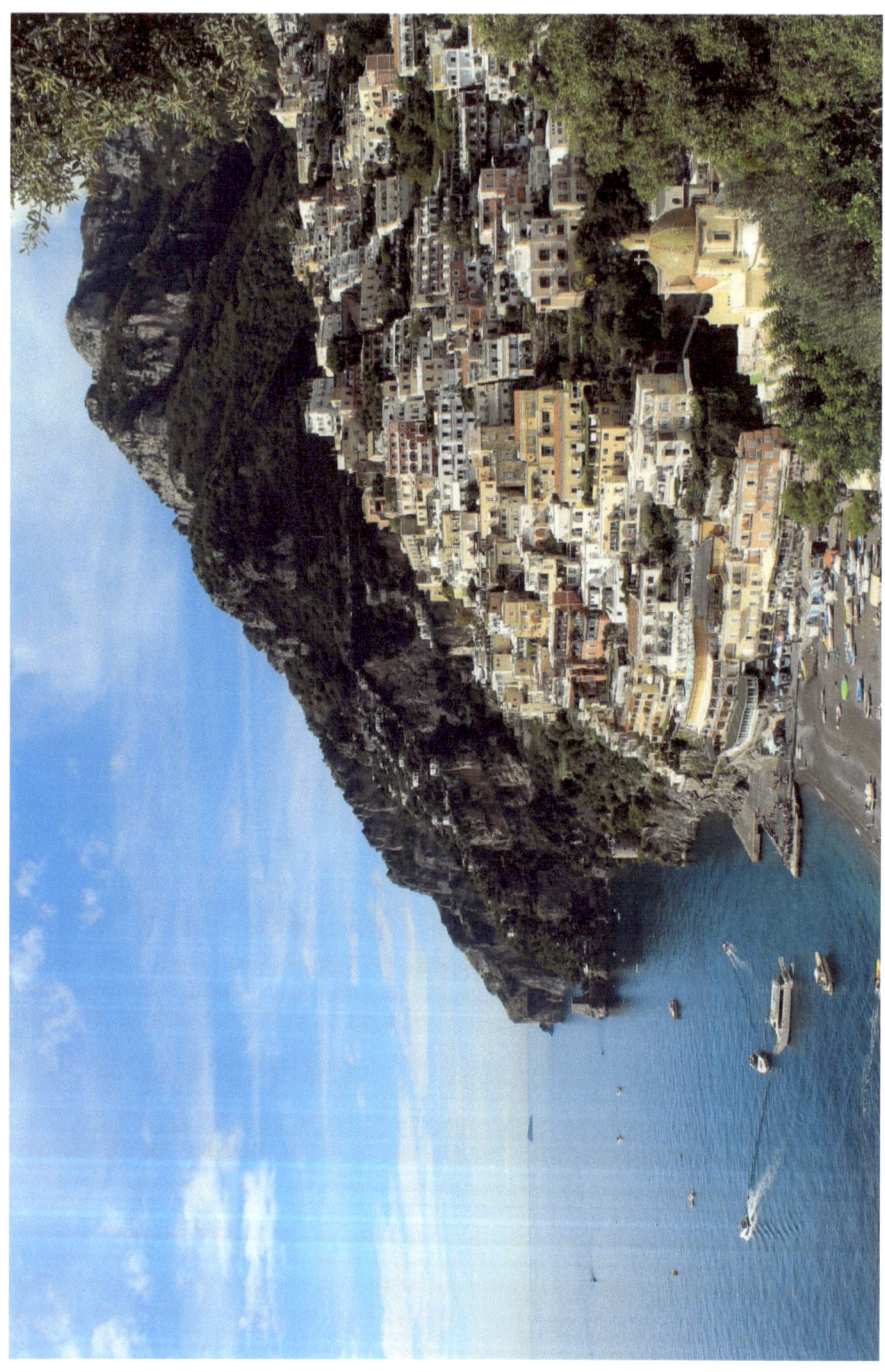

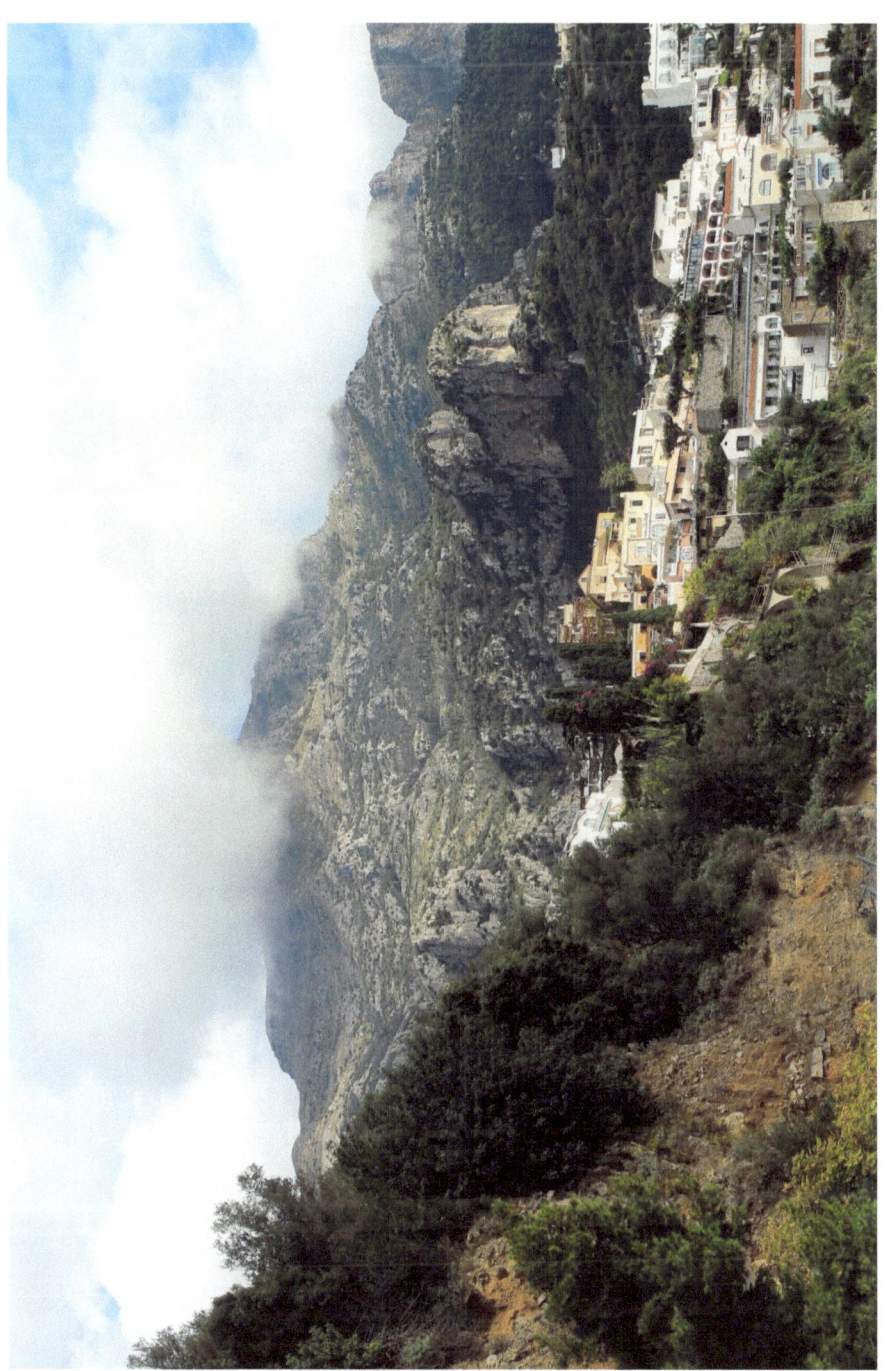

© Anna Castiglioni, 29

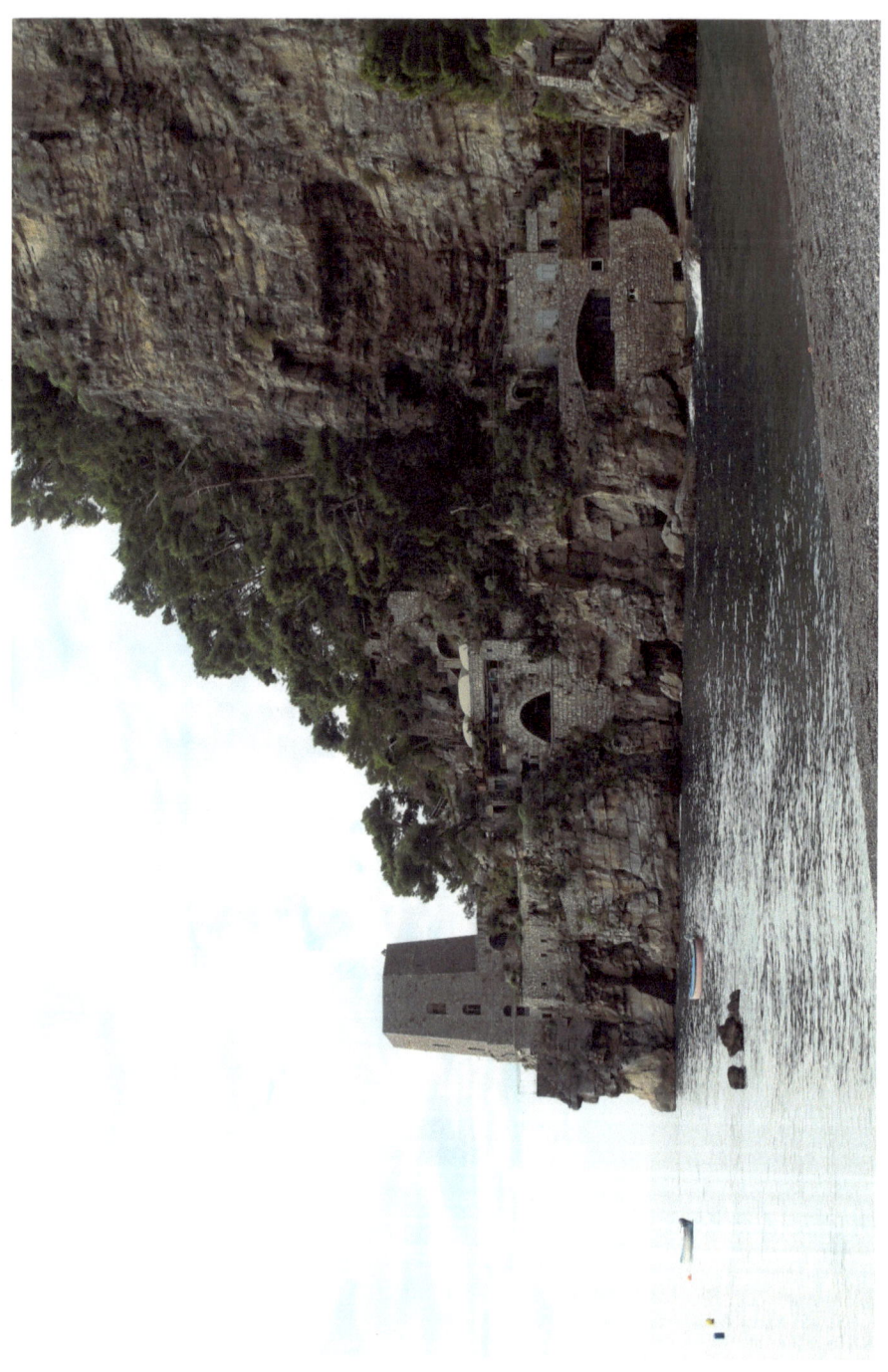

Positano, Amalfi Coast

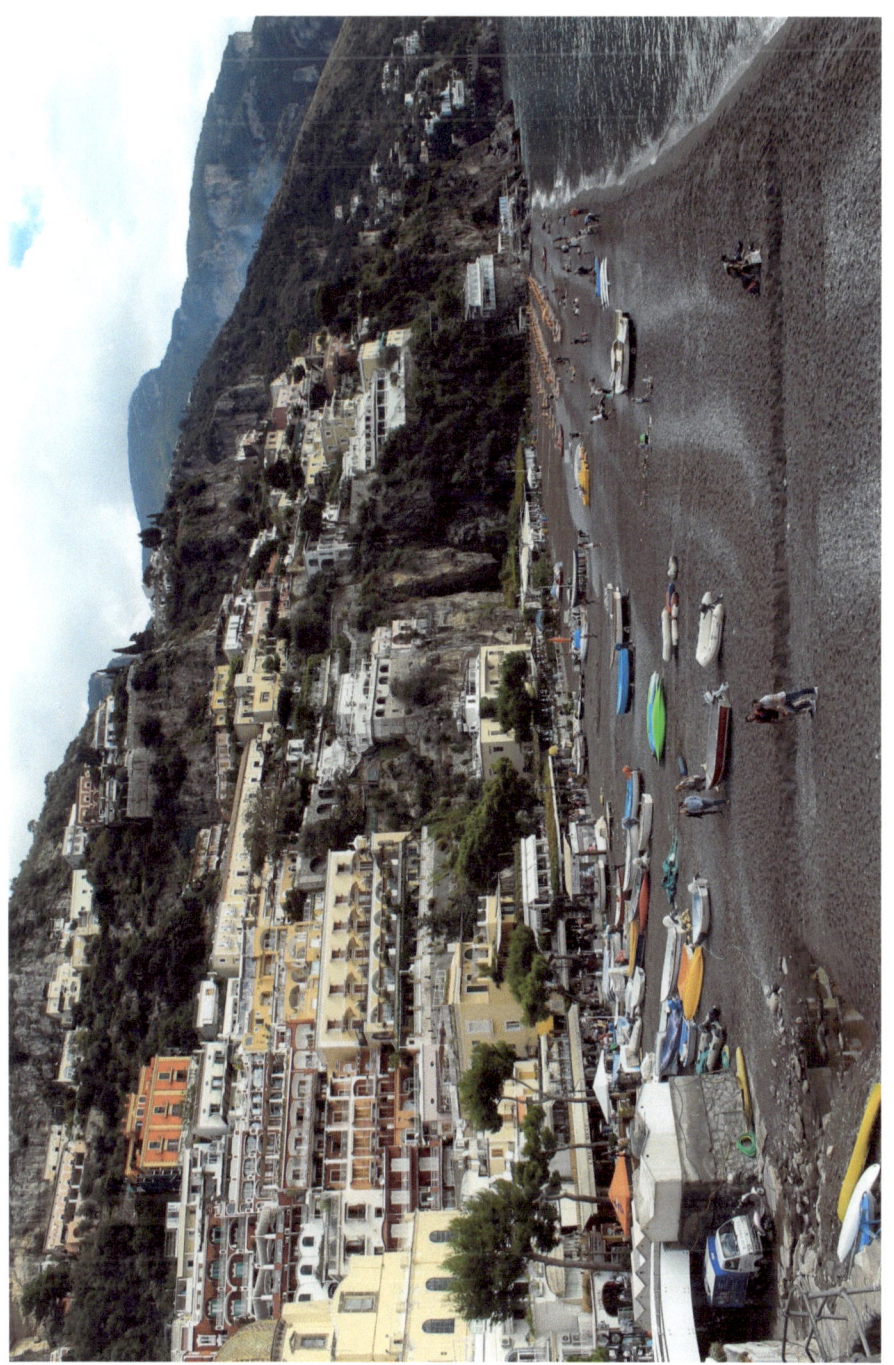

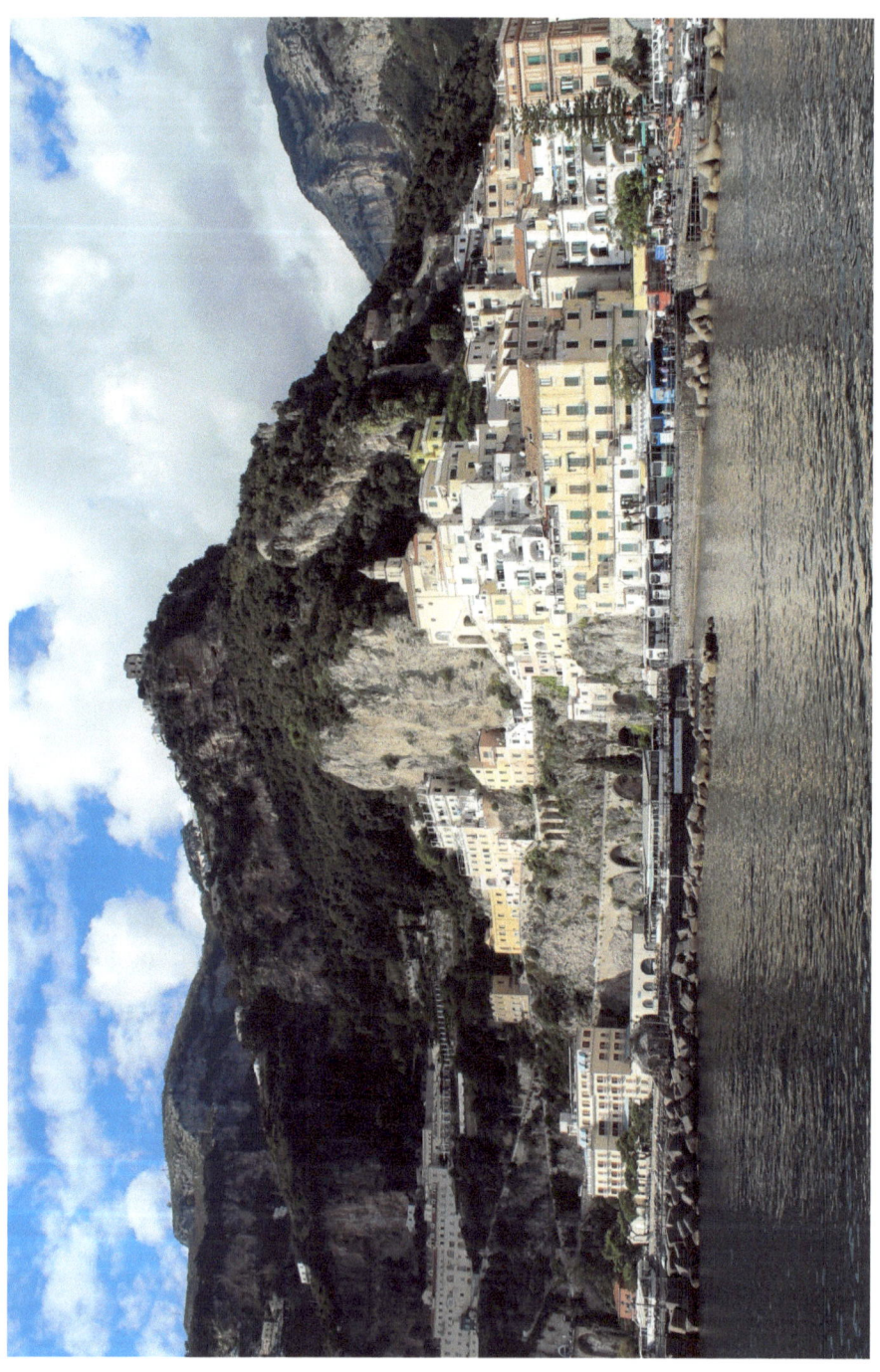

Ravello, Amalfi Coast

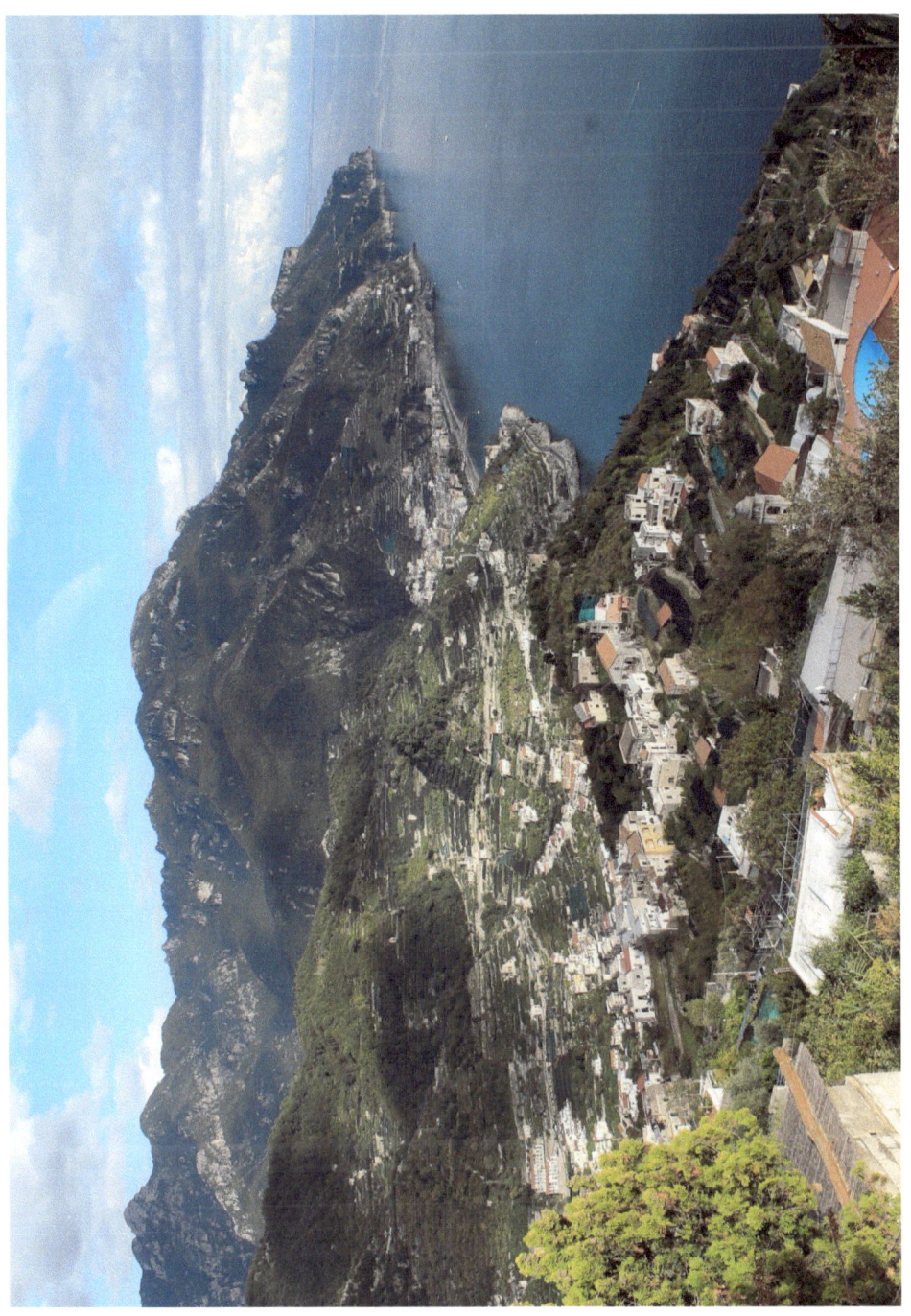

Also by Anna Castiglioni

La Viaggiatrice (The Traveler):
Backpacking Italy
A personal account of Italy,
Italian travel words and phrases, travel and adventure tips.

Plan to Planted:
Landscaping Your Home in Southern California
Professional tips for planning and designing your yard or garden.

Newbies Guide to Modding Skyrim:
Tips and Tricks for the Creation Kit
(A game design book)